Online Tips

FOR

DUMMIES®

Edited by Tamara Castleman

IDG Books Worldwide, Inc.
An International Data Group Company

Foster City, CA ✦ Chicago, IL ✦ Indianapolis, IN ✦ New York, NY

Online Tips For Dummies®

Published by

IDG Books Worldwide, Inc.

An International Data Group Company
919 E. Hillsdale Blvd.
Suite 400
Foster City, CA 94404
www.idgbooks.com (IDG Books Worldwide Web site)
www.dummies.com (Dummies Press Web site)

Library of Congress Catalog Card No.: 00-101004

ISBN: 0-7645-0727-3

Printed in the United States of America

10 9 8 7 6 5 4 3 2 1

1S/QR/QT/QQ/IN

Distributed in the United States by IDG Books Worldwide, Inc.

Distributed by CDG Books Canada Inc. for Canada; by Transworld Publishers Limited in the United Kingdom; by IDG Norge Books for Norway; by IDG Sweden Books for Sweden; by IDG Books Australia Publishing Corporation Pty. Ltd. for Australia and New Zealand; by TransQuest Publishers Pte Ltd. for Singapore, Malaysia, Thailand, Indonesia, and Hong Kong; by Gotop Information Inc. for Taiwan; by ICG Muse, Inc. for Japan; by Intersoft for South Africa; by Eyrolles for France; by International Thomson Publishing for Germany, Austria and Switzerland; by Distribuidora Cuspide for Argentina; by LR International for Brazil; by Galileo Libros for Chile; by Ediciones ZETA S.C.R. Ltda. for Peru; by WS Computer Publishing Corporation, Inc., for the Philippines; by Contemporanea de Ediciones for Venezuela; by Express Computer Distributors for the Caribbean and West Indies; by Micronesia Media Distributor, Inc. for Micronesia; by Chips Computadoras S.A. de C.V. for Mexico; by Editorial Norma de Panama S.A. for Panama; by American Bookshops for Finland.

For general information on IDG Books Worldwide's books in the U.S., please call our Consumer Customer Service department at 800-762-2974. For reseller information, including discounts and premium sales, please call our Reseller Customer Service department at 800-434-3422.

For information on where to purchase IDG Books Worldwide's books outside the U.S., please contact our International Sales department at 317-596-5530 or fax 317-572-4002.

For consumer information on foreign language translations, please contact our Customer Service department at 1-800-434-3422, fax 317-572-4002, or e-mail rights@idgbooks.com.

For information on licensing foreign or domestic rights, please phone +1-650-653-7098.

For sales inquiries and special prices for bulk quantities, please contact our Sales department at 800-762-2974 or write to the address above.

For information on using IDG Books Worldwide's books in the classroom or for ordering examination copies, please contact our Educational Sales department at 800-434-2086 or fax 317-572-4005.

For press review copies, author interviews, or other publicity information, please contact our Public Relations department at 650-653-7000 or fax 650-653-7500.

For authorization to photocopy items for corporate, personal, or educational use, please contact Copyright Clearance Center, 222 Rosewood Drive, Danvers, MA 01923, or fax 978-750-4470.

About the Authors

Reva Basch: Author of *Researching Online For Dummies,* published by IDG Books Worldwide, Inc., Reva Basch is a writer, editor, and consultant to the online industry. She operated her own online research business for more than 10 years. Prior to that, she was vice president and director of research at Information on Demand, a pioneering independent research company in Berkeley, California. She is a frequent speaker on topics related to information retrieval, virtual communities, the Internet and the World Wide Web, and has keynoted at international conferences in Australia, Scandinavia, and the United Kingdom, as well as Canada and the U.S.

Stephanie Becker: An Emmy Award-nominated television producer for NBC News, Stephanie Becker is co-author of *eBay For Dummies* (with Roland Woerner and Marsha Collier), published by IDG Books Worldwide, Inc. Her essays as Gadget Gal have appeared both in *Gadget Guru Guide Magazine* and on the Web. She is an avid cyclist and has several unique collections, including refrigerator magnets, momentos from catastrophes around the world, and dust bunnies.

Marsha Collier: A multi-tasking professional who uses all aspects of graphics in her advertising business, The Collier Company, Marsh Collier is also co-author of *eBay For Dummies* (with Roland Woerner and Stephanie Becker), published by IDG Books Worldwide, Inc. In her spare time, she's mastered the art of eBay and has over 600 positive feedback comments. Using her ability to spot trends, she continues to buy and sell on eBay, while also winning awards for her achievements in advertising and for her work in the community.

April Leigh Helm: President of Toolbox Internet Marketing Services, Inc., editor and maintainer of the *Journal of Online Genealogy,* and co-managing editor of *Genealogical Computing* magazine, April Leigh Helm is also co-author of *Genealogy Online For Dummies* (with Matthew Helm), published by IDG Books Worldwide, Inc. April spoke at GENTECH97 and has lectured on genealogy and other topics for various conferences and groups. She holds a B.S. in Journalism and an Ed.M. in Higher Education Administration from the University of Illinois at Urbana-Champaign.

Matthew Helm: Co-author of *Genealogy Online For Dummies* (with April Leigh Helm), published by IDG Books Worldwide, Inc., Matthew Helm is also Director of Online Editorial Content at *Ancestry.com;* Executive Vice President and Chief

Technology Officer for Toolbox Internet Marketing Services Inc.; publisher of the *Journal of Online Genealogy;* and co-managing editor of *Genealogical Computing* magazine. He is the creator and maintainer of Helm's Genealogy Toolbox, Helm/Helms Family Research Page, and a variety of other World Wide Web sites. Matthew has spoken at GENTECH96, GENTECH97, and Illinois State Genealogical Society conferences and has lectured on genealogy to various other groups. Matthew holds an A.B. in History and an M.S. in Library and Information Science from the University of Illinois at Urbana-Champaign.

Greg Holden: Founder and president of a small business called Stylus Media — a group of editorial, design, and computer professionals who produce both print and electronic publications — Greg Holden is also the author of *Internet Auctions For Dummies*, published by IDG Books Worldwide, Inc. He still can't drive by a sign for a garage sale or flea market without stopping to take a gander at the merchandise, but online auctions have helped him add hard-to-find items to his collections of pens, cameras, radios, and hats.

Julie Adair King: Julie Adair King, author of *Digital Photography For Dummies*, 3rd Edition, published by IDG Books Worldwide Inc., is also the author of *Adobe PhotoDeluxe For Dummies* and has contributed to many other books on digital imaging and computer graphics, including *CorelDRAW 7 For Dummies*, *PageMaker 6 For Dummies*, and *Macworld Photoshop 4 Bible*. She is also the author of *WordPerfect Suite 7 For Dummies, Corel WordPerfect Suite 8 For Dummies, Corel WordPerfect 2000 For Dummies,* and *Microsoft PhotoDraw 2000 For Dummies.*

Noah Vadnai: Since his travel-filled childhood, Noah Vadnai (author of *Travel Planning Online For Dummies,* 2nd Edition, published by IDG Books Worldwide, Inc.) has never been one to pass on the opportunity for a good trip. Noah has worked as a tree surgeon, a film and video production lackey, a photo editor for the Associated Press, and as the Travel Channel Producer for NetGuide, an online Internet directory and guide.

Roland Woerner: An Emmy Award-nominated producer and writer for NBC's *The Today Show*, Roland Woerner enjoys writing and producing segments exploring the world of technology and pop culture. In his spare time, the co-author of *eBay For Dummies*, (with Stephanie Becker and Marsha Collier) published by IDG Books Worldwide Inc., enjoys going on adventures with his daughters, flying airplanes, driving boats, and collecting lunchboxes and TV memorabilia.

Publisher's Acknowledgments

We're proud of this book; please register your comments through our IDG Books Worldwide Online Registration Form located at http://my2cents.dummies.com.

Some of the people who helped bring this book to market include the following:

Acquisitions, Editorial, and Media Development

Custom Development Editor:
Tamara S. Castleman

Editorial Director: Mary C. Corder

Editorial Assistant: Candace Nicholson, Beth Parlon

Product Marketing Manager:
Melisa Duffy

Production

Project Coordinator: Melissa Stauffer

Layout and Graphics: Joe Bucki, Barry Offringa, Tracy Oliver, Michael A. Sullivan, Dan Whetstine

Proofreader: Brian Massey

Indexer: Sharon Hilgenberg

General and Administrative

IDG Books Worldwide, Inc.: John Kilcullen, CEO

IDG Books Technology Publishing Group: Richard Swadley, Senior Vice President and Publisher; Walter Bruce III, Vice President and Associate Publisher; Joseph Wikert, Associate Publisher; Mary Bednarek, Branded Product Development Director; Mary Corder, Editorial Director; Barry Pruett, Publishing Manager; Michelle Baxter, Publishing Manager

IDG Books Consumer Publishing Group: Roland Elgey, Senior Vice President and Publisher; Kathleen A. Welton, Vice President and Publisher; Kevin Thornton, Acquisitions Manager; Kristin A. Cocks, Editorial Director

IDG Books Internet Publishing Group: Brenda McLaughlin, Senior Vice President and Publisher; Diane Graves Steele, Vice President and Associate Publisher; Sofia Marchant, Online Marketing Manager

IDG Books Production for Dummies Press: Debbie Stailey, Associate Director of Production; Cindy L. Phipps, Manager of Project Coordination, Production Proofreading, and Indexing; Tony Augsburger, Manager of Prepress, Reprints, and Systems; Laura Carpenter, Production Control Manager; Shelley Lea, Supervisor of Graphics and Design; Debbie J. Gates, Production Systems Specialist; Robert Springer, Supervisor of Proofreading; Kathie Schutte, Production Supervisor

Dummies Packaging and Book Design: Patty Page, Manager, Promotions Marketing

♦

The publisher would like to give special thanks to Patrick J. McGovern, without whom this book would not have been possible.

♦

Contents at a Glance

Table of Contents

Introduction

●●●

*F*or the strong of heart, the Internet can be an exciting adventure in which you jump from site to site quicker than Tarzan can grab a tree vine. However, most people find the Internet more like walking through alligator-infested waters — a great thrill if you make it across, but harrowing all the way. Many times, the Internet can be daunting at best; frustrating enough to make you use words your mom wouldn't like at worst.

If you can identify with the consternation — and swearing — that often comes from trying to navigate the Internet, then you've come to the right book. *Online Tips For Dummies* offers a treasure trove of ideas, hints, and suggestions for having fun, researching, and saving money on the Internet.

After reading this book, you'll be amazed at how well you can move around in the Internet jungle. (If you have a sudden urge to beat your chest and do the Tarzan yell, just make sure that your neighbors aren't watching.)

Why You Need This Book

You need this book because as the days grow longer, so does your "to do" list — vacations, family reunions, spring cleaning, and many other activities can make the spring and summer months downright exhausting. Technology, specifically that little thing called the Internet, *can* help, but only if you know where to go and what to do. This book helps you enjoy the spring and summer months by showing you how to use the Internet to the fullest — from vacation and reunion planning to selling garage sale fodder via Internet auctions. This book helps you get rid of the hassles, giving you a little more time in the hammock. Enjoy!

How to Use This Book

We're assuming that you want to spend time on the Internet, not with a book, so like all the other titles in the *For Dummies* series, you can start anywhere, read as little or as much as you want, and come away able to do some task better. Of course, if you can't get enough of this information and want to read from cover to cover you're certainly free to do so. It's your book — we're not going to tell you to put it down if you don't want to. And while we're on the subject of this being your book, feel free to write in it, highlight it, and — if you're feeling particularly generous — share the information with your family and friends.

How This Book Is Organized

This book is organized into three parts. The first part shows you how to use the Internet to get to places and connect with people; the second part tells you how to find things online. Part III gives you tools to save you time and money on the Internet.

Part I: Places to Go, People to See

The Internet is a fantastic device for checking out vacation destinations and making all kinds of reservations — air, hotel, car rental, and so on. The first chapter helps you decide where you may want to go. You get valuable sightseeing information, and suggestions for several types of vacations. After you decide where you're going, Chapter 2 tells you how to make your reservations — hassle-free — online. If you're planning on attending a family reunion or are interested in visiting your ancestors' old stomping grounds, Chapter 3 gives you information on finding and taking advantage of family reunions, as well as tips for conducting your research.

Part II: Things to Do

Few things can spoil a vacation quicker than unpredictable weather — except maybe a spouse who refuses to ask for directions. Chapter 4 shows you how to get weather forecasts the world over. This chapter also explains the great mapping features that the Internet offers. If your summer vacation plans involve cleaning out the attic, basement, or garage, Chapter 5 tells you how to turn your trash into money in your pocket. Who knows, you may even earn enough to hire someone else to do the cleaning while you go to Disneyland!

Part III: The Part of Tens

Every *For Dummies* book has a Part of Tens. This part always includes a few chapters that offer ten — give or take — quick tidbits of information to help you on your way. *Online Tips For Dummies* is no exception. Chapter 6 provides ten search engines that you can use to find the information you need quickly and efficiently. Chapter 7 offers a handful of money-saving tips via the Internet.

Icons Used in This Book

Throughout this book, you'll see these little pictures off to the side. We call these pictures icons, and every icon points to something special. Here's what each symbol means:

Simply stated, this icon points to information that you may want to remember. Think of this icon as a visual highlighter. If you agree, you may want to use a traditional highlighter on these paragraphs.

When you see this icon, it means that we're giving you a handy-dandy scrap of information to use to your advantage. These tips may save you time, money, and sanity.

Despite the little bomb ticking away, this icon is actually pretty helpful. The warning icon emphasizes information that may cause you grief, cost you money, or both.

Where to Go from Here

Decide what matters most to you, and flip to that part of the book. Or start right in with the first page. For additional information on the topics covered in this sampler book, check out the following titles, all published by IDG Books Worldwide, Inc.:

- *The Internet For Dummies*, 7th Edition (by John R. Levine, Carol Baroudi, and Margaret Levine Young)

- *E-mail For Dummies*, 2nd Edition (by John R. Levine, Carol Baroudi, Margaret Levine Young, and Arnold Reinhold)

- *Travel Planning Online For Dummies*, 2nd Edition (by Noah Vadnai)

- *Genealogy Online For Dummies* (by Matthew L. Helm and April Leigh Helm)

- *eBay For Dummies* (by Roland Woerner, Stephanie Becker, and Marsha Collier)

- *Digital Photography For Dummies*, 3rd Edition (by Julie Adair King)

- *Internet Directory For Dummies*, 3rd Edition (by Brad Hill)

Wherever you start, however you decide to use this book, please have fun on your Internet travels!

Part I

Places to Go, People to See

"I love these online travel tips, like how not to look like a tourist. Imagine – I was gonna get off the plane in India with a goofy camera around my neck."

In this part . . .

*T*his part is all about making connections on a budget.
We show you how to choose a vacation spot — and
maybe discover some vacation ideas you've never considered. Then, we connect you with the best travel agent you
can ask for — you! Family is often a big part of travel
plans, so we also give you some information on locating
family reunions and doing genealogical research.

After reading this part, your clicking finger will be itching to
choose an exotic locale, book a flight and a hotel, and examine the apples on your family tree.

Chapter 1

Investigating Your Destination Online

*T*he Internet makes planning and researching a vacation almost as much fun as the vacation itself. In fact, with loads of graphics and the most up-to-date information, the Internet makes the search for information a virtual vacation in itself. This chapter gives you the tools you need to start planning a trip by yourself or one with your family. If resorts or cruises are more up your alley, you can also find information on using the Internet to find *the* resort or *the* cruise that will make you the envy of the office.

Destinations 'R' Us

In the past few years, many sites have been developed to guide travelers to destinations around the globe. You can find quality destination information primarily at three types of sites:

✔ Guidebook sites that complement a line of printed travel literature, such as the Lonely Planet guidebooks (www.lonelyplanet.com), shown in Figure 1-1.

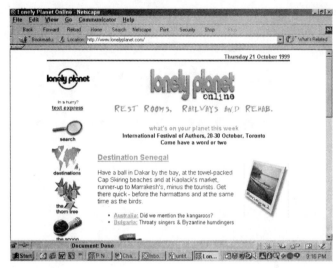

Figure 1-1: Lonely Planet Online helps you plan travel on a budget.

✔ Destination directories that are used as guides to the vast destination information on the Internet — City.Net (`city.net`) is one of the best.

✔ Full service online travel agencies often have complete online guidebooks as part of their sites — LeisurePlanet (`www.leisureplanet.com/TravelGuides/Travelguide.asp`) is a good example.

None of these types of guides are inherently superior to the other. A combination of all three gives you the best feel for the destination. If you always try to travel on the cheap, then you may want to start with Lonely Planet Online, guides that are designed for independent travelers on a budget. These guides also have good lists of Web links, for further researching.

If you don't know the first thing about a potential destination, start with a well-established, professional guide that can provide an overview, and then move on to smaller, non-commercial guides that can provide more focused and diverse info.

Online guides with books to match

If you're an experienced traveler, you may have a line of guidebooks that you use and have grown to trust. The good news is, your esteemed series of travel literature is probably published in one form or another on the Web. The bad news is, your computer is really heavy and not very fun to travel with.

Seriously, virtually every successful travel series has a Web site; some offer more free information than others.

Pointing You in the Right Direction: Destination Directories

Editors who are experts on travel resources on the Web compile online destination directories. These wonderful people spend all their time scouring the Web for the best resources and then cataloging them so you can access the solid information quickly and easily.

A good destination directory points you to a large variety of sites, all of which have been deemed worthwhile for a traveler researching a trip or vacation. Destination directories lead you to many diverse types of sites, including the following:

- Official country sites (governmental sites, visa, customs and passport info, and so on)
- Maps and weather information sites
- Culture and language information sites
- Lodging sites
- General travel and tourism sites

By using destination directories as a starting point, you always know where to quickly find destination info for any country or city. After you have a few good starting points, you can easily surf on to more related sites by using links. When you find a good piece of information, save it to compile your own guidebook. Following are great resources to use when you want to find quality Web sites that pertain to a destination:

- **City.Net:** Excite's City.Net (city.net) has listings for over 5,000 destinations. You can either search for a specific destination or browse the listings by clicking the map of the world. The top of each guide page has links that move you through that specific guide page.

- **NetGuide's TravelGuide:** NetGuide (www.netguide. com/Travel) is a guide to the best content on the Internet. The travel section has an ever-expanding list of destinations in the section called Destinations — how's that for irony? Click your destination and NetGuide presents you with a short article that contains links to noteworthy and valuable sites about that country or city. Within each article about a destination are hand-picked links to outstanding destination guides on the Web. The article also describes what to expect from each site, so you don't waste time surfing to sites that won't provide the travel guidance you're looking for.

- **The TravelPage:** The TravelPage (www.travelpage. com/dest.htm), Figure 1-2, is a comprehensive resource for travelers, developing original travel content as well as pointing you to other sites that provide travel information.

- **Yahoo! Travel Directory:** Almost every site worth its server has a listing on this king of Web directories. After clicking Travel on the main Yahoo! (www.yahoo.com/ Recreation/Travel/) page, go to the Regional section to find listings for countries and cities.

Figure 1-2: The TravelPage home page offers lots of useful information.

Planning Family Vacations Online

Whether you want to pack the family into the minivan and drive to an amusement park or make reservations at Disney World, start your planning with the Internet.

Starting with Yahoo!

If you're just trolling for family travel ideas, begin your research at Yahoo! (www.yahoo.com). All the places that kids like to visit are represented on Yahoo! — zoos, national parks, sports arenas, and so on. Go to the Travel category (www.yahoo.com/Recreation/Travel) and then click Family Travel. You find only about a dozen links here, which serve as a starting point to research family trips.

Yahoo! also has a category specifically listing amusement and theme parks (www.yahoo.com/Entertainment/Amusement_ and_Theme_Parks/) — a terrific way for your family to know what to expect from the park. Nearly every park with a Web presence has a listing here.

Kidding around — family vacation helpers

If you're traveling with children, you may find the following sites helpful:

- **The Family.com travel category page:** Family.com (http://family.go.com), Figure 1-3, is a Disney site, so you know they understand kids. But the site also knows parents and their travel planning needs. The featured stories at this site mostly deal with trips in the U.S., but the information is usually timely with regard to the season.

- **Travel with Kids from the Mining Co.:** The Travel with Kids page at the Mining Co. (travelwithkids. miningco.com/), features links to all sorts of family travel oriented info. The Travel with Kids section has terrific links organized by category, including budget travel, car trips, fun places with kids, and vacation ideas.

Figure 1-3: Family.com is a Disney site, and Disney knows children.

Resorting to Resorts

Most established resorts have a Web site that you can visit to check out prices, amenities, and photos. A Web site offers more depth than any paper brochure. The following sites are a sampling of the resorts you can find through Yahoo! or any of the other major search engines.

Club Med online

Club Med (www.clubmed.com), Figure 1-4, is perhaps the most well-known of all-inclusive resort chains. If you're considering a Club Med vacation, the Club Med Web site is a mandatory part of your visit. The site is extremely easy to use, if a bit slow to load.

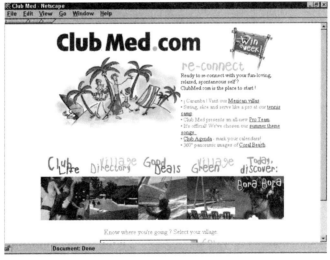

Figure 1-4: Resorting to the Club Med Web site is a good idea.

Sandals Resorts

Sandals Resorts (www.sandals.com), an "ultra-inclusive" experience, are for couples only. One price pays for everything at Sandals' dozen or so locations. After all, what's more romantic than never having to whip out the credit card to pay for anything? (If you're in doubt about the romantic nature of these one-price-for-love vacations, check out the Romantic Testimonials. This section offers first-hand experiences from real-life couples. It also has advice on how to plan your Sandals honeymoon or "Weddingmoon," as Sandals calls it.)

Select a resort by choosing an island (Sandals has resorts on four Caribbean islands) or by clicking directly on the resort name that interests you. Photos of each resort help with your selection. The Sandals site also helps you find a travel agent to book your trip (if you live in North America). Enter your zip code for the United States or select a city if you live in Canada. (If you live anywhere else, you're out of luck). The database finds expert Sandals agents right in your neighborhood.

Going Cruising

With all the cruise lines operating today, the Internet is a remarkable resource for researching and choosing cruises. You can check out a specific cruise line's Web page (they almost all have one) or you can conduct research on one of the various sites that are devoted to cruising. The Internet is also a great means of connecting with experienced cruisers who have firsthand knowledge of many different ships.

Finding the official cruise line sites

All the major cruise lines now have an online presence to promote their cruises; start researching a cruise on these official sites.

To locate the official site of the cruise line you're interested in, you can enter the name of the cruise line into a search engine such as Lycos (www.lycos.com), Infoseek (www.infoseek.com), or HotBot (hotbot.lycos.com). You can also use a travel site that maintains a link list of cruise lines Web sites. For example, the Travel Page's Cruise Page (www.travelpage.com/cruise.htm) has an exhaustive listing of official cruise line sites, reviews of boats, and other sites relevant to cruises.

Not surprisingly, the successful cruise lines tend to have better Web sites than their competitors:

✔ **Royal Caribbean Cruise Line**: Royal Caribbean Cruise Line (www.rccl.com), Figure 1-5, is one of the most popular and successful cruise operators in the world. And the line doesn't just cruise the Caribbean, as a visit to its Web site quickly reveals. The Royal Caribbean site illustrates all of its pages with vivid photography and descriptions, making your decision on which ship to choose much easier. Captain Steubing would approve.

Figure 1-5: The Royal Caribbean Cruise Line Web site is fit for a monarch.

✔ **Carnival Cruise Line:** The Carnival Cruise Line site (www.carnival.com) greets you with an animation of a cruise ship moving slowly across a beautiful background. If this scene isn't enough to get you in the mood to cruise, click any of the following buttons for even more enticement:

- **Ships:** Takes a look at the Carnival fleet. Click the boat's name to explore its features — photos of each area of the boat accompany short descriptions of its features.

- **Cruises:** Here you find the cruises organized by region. The site may, however, refer you to an official Carnival travel agent for pricing information.

- **Fun:** Examine all the fun aspects of a Carnival cruise — spas, food, nightlife, and more.

- **Contact information:** This section provides e-mail addresses for reservations, pricing, and guest relations.

- **FAQ:** Answers to frequently asked questions about Carnival cruises.

✔ **Norwegian Cruise Line:** The Norwegian Cruise Line page (www.ncl.com), Figure 1-6, has a very attractive design and is easy to navigate, even without a first mate. The following features proffer a cargohold-full of information:

Figure 1-6: The easy-to-navigate Norwegian Cruise Line site.

- **Destinations:** Explore all the places that Norwegian cruises go.

- **Fleet:** Click the big ship on the home page and then select a boat to learn about its amenities.

- **Latitudes:** Latitudes is the NCL loyalty program for repeat guests. If you've been on at least one NCL cruise, you're eligible to become a member. Benefits include special promotions, a periodic newsletter, and more.

- **Theme Cruises:** Each year, NCL plans special cruises that have a sports or musical theme. Check here for the dates and info.

- **More Info:** Find out about NCL's additional vacation offerings.

- **Special Offers:** Look here for cruise bargains on NCL cruise packages.

- **News:** Check out the latest NCL press releases and company info.

Utilizing independent cruise resources

In addition to the official cruise line sites, many Web sites can help you plan a cruise. The resources you find at these independent sites differ from what you get at an official site in the following ways:

- ✔ You get links to many official cruise line sites (including lesser known lines) as well as links to Web pages about cruising.

- ✔ You can read critical commentary and reviews of specific cruises and boats.

- ✔ You have means of connecting with travelers who have been on cruises.

- ✔ You can find out about cruise discounts for a variety of cruise lines.

- ✔ You can read up-to-date news from the cruise industry.

Booking a cruise online?

None of the major cruise lines allows you to reserve and *book* (pay for) cruises online due, in part, to the complexity of cruise reservations — you have to reserve cabin types, ships, dates, routes, packages, and so on. Truthfully, these complexities are difficult enough that you're better off talking to a person. However, if you really want to book a cruise online, Preview Travel (www.previewtravel.com) allows customers to actually reserve and book a cruise completely online.

Cruise sites that aren't affiliated with any specific cruise line make valuable bookmarks for both novice and experienced cruisers because these independent sites contain unbiased information about a variety of cruises. Following are a few of the best:

✔ **Travel Page Cruise Page:** As a comprehensive cruise resource, the Travel Page Cruise Page (www.cruisepage. com), Figure 1-7, has links to nearly every cruise line on the planet, discount cruise information, and reviews of over 9,000 cruises — all free for the asking. You can also check out the cruise bargains in the left-hand column, which has current listings for the best in cruise values. Sign up to receive the free, weekly e-mail newsletter that details the latest cruise news and discounts.

Figure 1-7: The Travel Page Cruise page sets you sailing.

✔ **CruiseFun:** CruiseFun (www.cruisefun.com), Figure 1-8, offers very current info about a wide range of cruises and ships. Travel Incorporated, an Illinois-based travel agency, produces this site as well as Cruise News Daily (www.reply.net/clients/cruise/cnd.html), a listing of the latest cruise news happenings. Consult CruiseFun for the latest cruise news and passenger reviews, or click Cruise Search to find the perfect cruise for you, using criteria that you select.

Figure 1-8: The CruiseFun Web site is up-to-date and full of cruise news.

✔ **CruiseOpinion.com:** With a database of over 1,300 reviews written by actual cruisers, CruiseOpinion.com (www.cruiseopinion.com), gives you unedited, first-hand knowledge of specific boats and itineraries. You can read reviews for specific ships, as well as offer your own reviews of your past cruises.

Chapter 2

Using Your Computer as Your Travel Agent

• •

• •

*I*f you've ever booked a flight or hotel through a travel agent, you may have been left wondering whether you really did get the best possible rate. With the Internet, you can put that question to rest once and for all. Many sites allow you to research and book online. You can also find some great bargains on the Web — some that your travel agent may not even know about! This chapter introduces you to the ins and outs of making reservations online.

Meet the Big Four Online Travel Agents

Since the advent of the Web, many online travel agencies have set up shop, each vying for a slice of the burgeoning online-booking pie. To some degree, the dust has settled, and four full-service online travel agencies (affectionately known as the Big Four) have risen to the top to establish themselves as the online booking sites to beat.

Each of these four major online travel agencies offers the following features that set them apart from other agencies:

- ✔ **Ease of use:** You shouldn't have to struggle to use a site's features the first time you visit.

- ✔ **Secure credit card transactions:** You can safely send your credit card and personal information to each of the Big Four sites. (Read the sidebar "Staying safe and secure online" in this chapter for more information on the security issues surrounding business on the Internet.)

- ✔ **Personal profiles:** To aid in the selection of the correct flight, the Big Four online agencies allow you to store a *travel profile*. When you log in, the site knows your preferred airport, preferred airlines, whether you fly mostly for business or pleasure, and how you take your coffee.

- ✔ **Low fare features:** The Big Four constantly develop new ways to keep you informed about low fares.

- ✔ **Access to living travel agents:** Although their fondest hope is that you book all your travel online, the Big Four also employ live travel agents that are available many hours a day via a toll-free phone number.

What can you do?

A full-service, online travel agency, such as any of the Big Four, performs many of the roles that you receive from a living agent, as well as a few additional services. They

- ✔ Research destinations, and then find and book flights.

- ✔ Compare prices, seats, routings, and track flights in progress.

- ✔ Provide information about discounts and incentives, and keep you up on travel news and events.

With all these amazing online travel features, you may think that you never need to speak to another offline travel agent. But ticketing air travel is a complex procedure. Many tickets have complicated restrictions that no piece of software can decipher. Travel agents spend years figuring out how to finesse computer systems and to understand the esoteric ticketing procedures; an astute agent's expertise can't be replaced by any automated system.

Who should use the Big Four?

While the Big Four have made terrific advances in the past couple years, online travel agents still work best for the following travelers:

- ✔ **Those traveling in the U.S. or Canada:** Due to the nature of the travel industry and the means by which domestic and international air tickets are priced, online travel agents function best for tickets to American and Canadian destinations.

- ✔ **Those traveling frequently:** If you travel frequently, booking your own tickets saves you tons of time.

- ✔ **Those participating in airline awards programs:** If you covet airline award miles the way some people love to gamble, booking online allows you to make sure that you fly with airlines that participate in your frequent flyer program.

Who are the Big Four?

These four sites have had enormous success in the past few years, and their established relationships with the powers-that-be in the travel industry make these the sites to use for the foreseeable future. Other online booking sites exist, but you can feel confident that when you use one of the Big Four sites, you're dealing with online agents who are highly professional and reputable.

Expedia

Microsoft's online travel agency, Expedia (expedia.msn.com), Figure 2-1, is a late entrant into the cadre of online agency super-sites, but it is certainly one of the finest on the Web. Expedia maintains a 24-hour customer service number (1-800-936-4500) for questions, but you must have an itinerary number to use the service.

The following cool features on Expedia can help you get good deals on flights:

- ✔ **Fare Tracker:** Keep an eye on the fares on up to three flight routes that interest you. Each week you receive an e-mail showing the best fares available for the given routes. Simply fill out the city pair (departure and destination cities) and then click Subscribe to Fare Tracker. You access the Fare Tracker from the main Travel Agent page.

✔ **Fare Compare:** Use this feature to search the database for the lowest published fares for a flight. But don't get too excited when you find a great price — many of these fares are unavailable for various reasons. To find the lowest published fares, click Lowest Published Fares link on the main Travel Agent page.

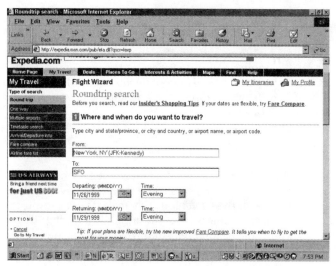

Figure 2-1: Expedia.com is Microsoft's online travel agency.

Internet Travel Network

In addition to its own fine site, Internet Travel Network (www.itn.net) — affectionately called ITN by travelers worldwide — has carved a niche for itself by becoming the booking site for many of the most popular travel sites on the Web, including CNN and American Express. This site provides another fine choice for booking flights (as well as hotels and cars) online. (ITN also has a 24-hour customer service center that you can call toll-free — from the U.S. and Canada — at 1-800-253-9822.) ITN allows you to book flights that originate from any country.

Many, many of the Web's most popular sites use ITN's reservation software. ITN is almost always involved anytime you come across a site that offers online travel reservations.

For your discount pleasure, ITN offers the following features, which you can access from the ITN home page:

✔ **Low Fare Ticker:** Opens a small browser window where low fares from your selected home airport continuously scroll by.

✔ **Fare Mail:** Go to the Fare Mail page and sign up to receive e-mail updates of the fares to destinations of your choosing. You can set Fare Mail to mail you as often as you'd like.

Preview Travel

Preview Travel (www.previewtravel.com), shown in Figure 2-2, puts an emphasis on user-friendliness — the site goes out of its way to make buying all kinds of travel products online an easy task. With Preview's many partnerships within the online and traditional travel industry, you're bound to see special travel promotions advertised on the site.

Figure 2-2: The user-friendly Preview Travel home page.

Travelocity

Travelocity (www.travelocity.com) — a descendant of the easySabre, the first online booking site — now ranks as one of the best known agencies on the Web.

Travelocity's database of fares is one of the largest and busiest, performing millions of reservations requests each day; unfortunately, the site's popularity sometimes makes Travelocity very busy and slow to use.

You can book flights that originate from any country with Travelocity. In terms of customer service, 24-hour phone service is unavailable, but they do provide an e-mail submittal form.

You may want to visit Travelocity's Flights Menu and sign up for the following features (the site tells you how to do so):

- ✔ **Departure/Arrival Times:** Gives access to the current info for nearly every airline, even if you don't know the flight number.

- ✔ **Flight Paging:** If you have an alphanumeric pager, Travelocity can page you when flights are delayed or canceled. The pager also displays gate and baggage claim info.

- ✔ **Flight Timetable:** Get schedules for almost every airline by entering your query into the search form and clicking Submit.

- ✔ **Fare Information:** Enter the appropriate airports and find out the current published fares between two points.

- ✔ **Fare Watcher E-mail:** Enter up to five pairs of cities you wish to have Travelocity monitor for fare information. The program notifies you via your e-mail account when the fares change by more than $25.

Get Travel Discounts by E-Mail

With the Internet's rapid growth, airlines, cruise lines, hotels, and other travel-product suppliers quickly realized that they could use the Internet to sell their unused inventory via e-mail at the last minute.

Staying safe and secure online

Does the idea of entering your credit card numbers and other sensitive information into a form on a Web page and clicking the Submit button leave you anxious? Well, relax. As long as the site you submit your credit card info to has *encryption,* a process that essentially encodes your information into a long code, a miscreant is hard-pressed to decode your credit card number and personal information.

Both the Netscape and Internet Explorer browsers make it easy for you to tell whether a site uses encryption:

✔ Look for a chain or padlock in the bottom, left-hand corner on Netscape browser versions 3.0 and 4.0.

✔ Look for a lock in the bottom, right-hand corner of Internet Explorer versions 3.0 and higher.

When the lock isn't broken, you're connected to a *secure server,* a piece of hardware that "Joe Hacker" can rarely break into. Basically, your information is as safe, if not safer, on a secure server than when you give your credit card number over the phone.

Rather than flying planes half full, the airlines much prefer to sell their empty seats at cut prices. To fill those empty seats, most airlines gladly send out a free, weekly e-mail newsletter containing deals on flights. Other suppliers offer similar newsletters that focus on hotels, vacation packages, and other products. These discounted fares come directly from the travel suppliers — airlines, hotels, and tour operators — so you won't find the deals listed at discount travel Web sites.

However, the only way to take advantage of these bargains is if your schedule is flexible and you're willing to fly at the last minute. For the most part, these deals only become available about a week prior to the departure dates. Most of the newsletter mailings go out on Wednesday because the airlines can't judge until the middle of the week how much inventory they have remaining, and thus know which tickets they should sell at cut rates.

You have to subscribe to these newsletters in order to get your foot in the online travel discount door. Follow these steps to subscribe:

1. **Visit the airline's official Web site.**

   You can find every airline's Web address by visiting a site called Airline Toll-Free Numbers and Web sites (www.princeton.edu/Main/air800.html).

2. **Find the link on the airline site's home page that leads to the newsletter subscription and discount information.**

   A few of the better known programs are American Airlines' NetSAAver fares, Continental Airlines' CO.O.L. Travel Specials, and Northwest Airlines' CyberSavers.

3. **Input your e-mail address, name, and perhaps some additional information into the form on the airline site.**

   Most airlines ask you for your home airport and then tailor your e-mail newsletter to reflect the available discounted fares that depart from your city. Some airlines, such as TWA, allow you to specify the routes that most interest you and then mail you fares each week for just those routes.

4. **Click a button to submit your newsletter request.**

   After you submit the info, you usually receive a confirmation e-mail to let you know that you're signed up. You begin receiving the newsletter on the next date of publication.

If you find that the discount e-mails just wind up as unread clutter in your mailbox, you can easily unsubscribe. Most newsletters include instructions at the end of each mailing on how to unsubscribe. Usually, you just send an e-mail to a certain address with the word UNSUBSCRIBE in the body of the message.

You must purchase any discounted fare you read about in an airline newsletter directly from the airline by either calling the reservation phone number or using the airline's Web-based reservation system. Act fast because these last-minute deals always get gobbled up very quickly.

Beware the fantastic deal

Some dishonest parties take advantage of travelers' desires to get good deals by luring them into scams with really great deals. Just as in conventional commerce, the online marketplace has its share of schemers and fraudulent businesses. To avoid these schemes, ask yourself these questions when you see a deal that seems too good to be true:

✔ **Does a well-known travel supplier maintain the Web site?** Do they belong to any of the travel industry trade organizations (the ASTA, CLIA, and so on); reputable vendors will always proudly display these memberships.

✔ **Why are they offering a discount on the product?** Giving something away for nothing isn't good business.

✔ **Is the product for sale actually available?** Occasionally, you may come across amazingly low airfares at discount travel sites. Upon closer inspection, however, these fares often have no availability.

Find Airfare Bargains on the Web

That's a pretty juicy heading, but before you salivate all over your keyboard, you should know no sure-fire method exists to get an airfare bargain every time you wish to fly for every route you wish to fly. You can, however, consistently find tasty fares if you know how and where to look, but you may have to be flexible with your times and destinations. The following methods can help you find that elusive travel bargain you're pining for.

Using discount online travel agencies

In addition to the Big Four online travel agencies (see the section "Meet the Big Four" earlier in this chapter), you can find online travel agencies that specialize in selling discounted airline tickets — and sometimes also cruises, vacation packages, and other travel products. (***Remember:*** The flights you find at these sites are often unavailable or have many restrictions.)

You can find terrific low fares and great vacation deals — just don't forget to read any and all fine print.)

Snaring rock-bottom airfare prices

Airtech.com (www.airtech.com/), Figure 2-3, specializes on getting flights on major carriers between the following regions:

- ✔ The United States to Europe
- ✔ Europe to the United States
- ✔ The United States to Mexico and the Caribbean
- ✔ San Francisco, Los Angeles, and Phoenix to Hawaii
- ✔ Hawaii to San Francisco, Los Angeles, and Phoenix

Here's the catch: You must provide Airtech.com with a window of time (usually about five days) during which you can travel (you may also need to be flexible with your departure, and sometimes arrival points). If you can deal with not knowing an exact departure date, Airtech.com will get you on a flight — for the cheapest possible fare. Also keep in mind that most of the prices that Airtech.com quotes apply only to one-way trips (except where noted otherwise).

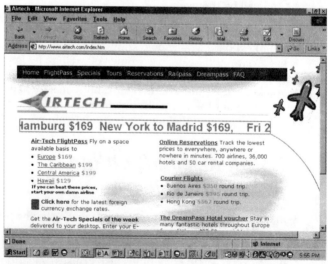

Figure 2-3: Airtech.com can save you money — if you have flexibility.

Electronic tickets (e-tickets)

The issuance of paperless tickets, or *e-tickets*, has become an extremely common occurrence for air travel in the United States and is becoming common elsewhere. Travelers can now reserve a flight by phone, travel agent, or online, and then show up at the airport with valid, government issued identification and collect their boarding pass — all without ever possessing a conventional paper ticket. The whole reservation is held in the computer system; you still get a receipt from the travel agent or airline, either by fax or by mail, but this receipt, although helpful, is not necessary to receive your boarding pass at the airport.

While you're at Airtech.com, check its other offerings for cheap hotels and other flight plans.

Finding bargains on official hotel sites

Every night, thousands and thousands of hotel beds go to sleep all by themselves, completely untouched, the sheets neatly made, and the bedtime mint uneaten. Hotel chains hate lonely beds, so they make deals on available rooms, beckoning potential guests to come and stay the night. The following sites (and this list is only a partial one) show just how far the major hotel chains are willing to go to get you into their beds:

- ✔ **Hilton Special Offers** (www.hilton.com/specials/index.html)**:** Tells you all about travel packages, special offers, and Hilton Value Rates at hotels across the globe.

- ✔ **Holiday Inn HOLIDEALS** (www.basshotels.com/holiday-inn)**:** Get the lowdown on the latest Holiday Inn promotions.

- ✔ **Hyatt Hot Deals** (www.hyatt.com/hotdeals/index.html)**:** Find special offers around the world, last-minute deals, and other promotions.

- ✔ **Marriott Hotel Fridays Promotion** (marriotthotels.com/friday/): Get 10 to 20 percent off at participating Marriott hotels each week.

- ✔ **Sheraton Hot Deals** (www.sheraton.com/hot_deals/index.html): Check in to see what the Sheraton is offering for guests.

Check with your favorite hotel's Web site before you make a reservation to see whether you can save some money. You're sure to make some lonesome bed very happy.

Chapter 3

Getting Your Family Together

● ●

In This Chapter

▶ Beginning a genealogy search

▶ Meeting, greeting, and researching through chats and queries

▶ Creating an electronic photo album

● ●

*T*he Internet makes staying in touch with family members scattered across the globe a "relatively" easy task. But the Internet is also a wonderful place to search for family members you didn't even know you had! This chapter explores genealogy on the Web and tells you how to find information and post queries on the Internet. After you reconnect with long-lost cousin Ernie, you may want to exchange photos, so the end of this chapter explains how to set up an electronic photo album.

Starting with What You Know

When attempting to geographically locate your ancestors, start by using any copies of records that you or someone else in the family has already collected. Your notes from interviews with family members, or from other resources you've found on your ancestors, most likely contain some information about locations where the family lived and hopefully the approximate time frames of when they lived there.

Chances are you have at least some notes with general statements (or recollections of stories you've heard), such as "Aunt Lola recalled stories about the old homestead in Fayette County, Kentucky." These stories give you a starting point.

Likewise, most public records that you've collected or someone else has given you — vital records, land records, military documents, and so on — provide at least two leads for you to use in tracking your family: the names of parents or witnesses to the event, and the date and place of the event (or at least the date and place of when and where the record was filed). Having this information can point you in the right direction of where to begin looking for other records to substantiate what you believe to be true about your ancestors. Knowing a name to look for in a particular place and time gets you on your way to seeking other records.

Scouring Directories and Newspapers

If you have a general idea of where your family lived at a particular time, but no conclusive proof, city and county directories and newspapers may help. (Census records are quite helpful for this purpose, too.) Directories and newspapers can help you confirm whether your ancestors indeed lived in a particular area and, in some cases, they can provide even more information than you expect.

Directories

Like today's telephone books, directories contained basic information about the persons who lived in particular areas, whether the areas were towns, cities, districts, or counties. Typically, the directory identified at least the head of the household and the location of the house. Some directories also included the names and ages of everyone in the household and occupations of any members of the household who were employed.

Unfortunately, no centralized resource on the Web contains transcriptions of directories or even an index to all directories that may exist on the Internet. Some sites can direct you to directories for particular geographic areas, but they're by no means universal. You can find a list of city directories for nearly 700 American towns and states that are available on microfilm at the City Directories at the Library of Congress Web page (www.kinquest.com/genealogy/resources /citydir.html). Local libraries also sometimes have large collections of city directories.

For tips on using city directories, see the following:

- ✔ "City Directories," by George Morgan (www.ancestry.com/columns/george/03-06-98.htm)

- ✔ "City Directories: Windows on the Past," by Myra Vanderpool Gormley (www.ancestry.com/columns /myra/Shaking_Family_Tree03-19-98.htm).

Some societies and associations have made a commitment to post on the Web the contents of directories for their areas or at least an index of what their libraries hold so that you know before you contact them whether they have something useful to you. To help you find out whether such a project exists for an area you're researching, use the location-specific search engine at Genealogy Portal.com (www.genealogyportal.com). This tool enables you to search the full text of several genealogical Web sites at once.

Uncle, I never knew ye

Morbid as it is, we have a true story that illustrates how helpful newspapers can be. A man was looking through newspapers for an obituary about one of his great-uncles. He knew when his great-uncle died but couldn't find mention of his death in the obituary section of the newspaper. As he set the newspaper down (probably in despair), the man glanced to the front page only to find a very graphic description of how this local man had been killed in a freak elevator accident.

And guess who that local man was? That's right, the man's great-uncle! The newspaper not only confirmed for the man that his great-uncle lived there, but also gave him more information than he ever expected.

Newspapers

Newspapers are helpful only if your ancestors did something that was newsworthy — but you'd be surprised at what was considered newsworthy in the past. Obituaries, birth and marriage announcements, public records of land transactions, advertisements, and gossip sections were all relatively common in newspapers of the past.

Finding online copies of those newspapers from the past is a challenge. Most of the newspaper sites currently on the Web are for contemporary publications. Here's what you're likely to find online pertaining to newspapers:

- ✔ **Indexes:** A variety of sites serve as indexes of newspapers that are available at particular libraries, archives, and universities. Most of these list the names and dates of the periodicals that are held in the newspaper or special collections. One such site is the Online Newspaper Indexes, available in the newspaper and current periodical reading room of the Library of Congress (lcweb.loc.gov/rr/news/npindex2.html).

- ✔ **Transcriptions:** A few sites contain actual transcriptions of newspaper articles, entire issues, and/or excerpts. Typically, the contents at these sites are limited to the topic and geographic interests of the person who transcribed the information and posted it for public access on the Web. One such site is Virtual Family Records Vault (www.vfamily.com/).

- ✔ **Collectors' issues for sale:** Although they don't provide online information directly from the newspaper for you to use in your genealogical pursuits, these sites can help you locate collectors' editions of newspapers and possibly even buy them online. For the services to be really useful to you as a genealogist, you have to know the date and place of the event you want to document (a newspaper name helps, too). One collector's site that may interest you is the Historic Newspaper Archives (www.historicnewspaper.com)

- ✔ **Online newspaper projects:** As people begin to recognize the important role newspapers play in recording history and the value of putting newspaper information on the Web, you'll see an increasing number of online projects to catalog or transcribe newspapers. The Web sites for these projects explain the purpose of the project, its current status, and how to find the newspapers if they've been transcribed or digitized and placed online. For example, you may want to check out the New York State Newspaper Project (`www.nysl.nysed.gov/nysnp/`), shown in Figure 3-1.

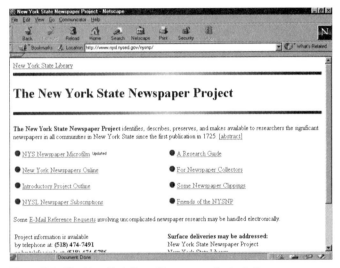

Figure 3-1: The New York State Newspaper Project site.

If you want to look for other newspaper sites, use a trusty comprehensive genealogical site.

Chatting Up a Room

Chat rooms are Internet sites where you can log in and participate in real-time (or with just a few seconds delay) conversations. A few chat rooms discuss genealogy specifically. Typically, the genealogy chat rooms (or in some cases, prearranged sessions) are hosted by or are available through the commercial Internet service providers — particularly America Online — or the Internet Relay Chat (IRC) network.

The IRC hosts several areas (called *channels*) where you can find discussions about genealogy. To access and use a chat channel on IRC, you have to use chat software. For more information about the genealogy-related chat channels, visit the Home Page for Genealogy on IRC (`www.genealogy.org/~jkatcmi/genealogy-irc/`). Not only does this home page tell you what's available, its FAQ (Frequently Asked Questions) section provides detailed instructions for downloading the chat software and joining chat channels as well.

Answering Your Surname Questions

Even if you can't find any surname-specific sites on your particular family, you still have hope! This hope comes in the form of queries. *Queries* are research questions that you post to a particular World Wide Web site, mailing list, or newsgroup, so that other researchers can help you solve your research problems. Often, other researchers have information that they haven't yet made available about a family, or they may have seen some information on your family even though it isn't a branch that they're actively researching.

World Wide Web queries

One of the quickest ways of reaching a wide audience with your query is through a query site on the World Wide Web. Following are some good sites to start with:

- ✔ **GenForum** (`genforum.genealogy.com`)
- ✔ **GenConnect** (`genconnect.rootsweb.com/index.html`)
- ✔ **FamilyHistory.com** (`www.familyhistory.com`)

Mailing list queries

Mailing lists are formed by groups of people who share common interests, whether those interests are in surnames, specific geographic areas, particular topics, or ethnic groups. A list consists of the e-mail addresses of every person who joins (subscribes to) the group.

Follow these steps to find and join a mailing list for your surname:

1. **Point your Web browser to** `members.aol.com/gfsjohnf/gen_mail.html` **and select the first letter of a surname you're interested in.**

   The letters appear near the bottom of the page.

2. **Scroll through the list and click one of the surname links on the page.**

   By scrolling through the list, you can see whether your surname is represented. Note that several mailing lists include variations of the surname as part of the scope of their discussions. So, even if the exact spelling of your surname doesn't appear in the list, skimming some of the surnames with similar spellings is a good idea.

3. **Follow the subscription instructions for your mailing list.**

   Typically, you can receive mailing lists in one of two ways. The first way, *mail mode,* simply forwards e-mail messages to you every time someone posts to the mailing list. Although this practice is fine for small mailing lists, you probably don't want hundreds of messages coming in individually — unless you like to have lots of e-mail sitting in your inbox. To avoid this problem, try the second way of receiving the mailing list — *digest mode.* Digest mode groups several messages together and then sends them out as one large message. Instead of receiving 30 messages a day, you may receive only two messages with the text of 15 messages in each.

4. **Start your e-mail program and subscribe to the mailing list.**

   Within a couple of minutes, you should receive a confirmation message welcoming you to the mailing list.

   Within the text of the confirmation messages that most mailing lists send is some valuable information that you want to hold on to for as long as you subscribe to the list — such as how to unsubscribe from the list, how to post messages to the list for others to read, and what format you should use for posting queries.

5. **Begin posting your own queries and responses to others' messages when you feel comfortable.**

Consider reading the messages without responding or posting your own messages — known as *lurking* — for a while. This way you can see what other messages look like and become familiar with the general culture of the list. After you get a feel for the structure and attitude of the messages, jump in and begin sending your own queries and messages!

Newsgroup queries

Another place where you can post queries is in a *newsgroup*. Newsgroups are similar to mailing lists in that you use e-mail to send a message that many people can read. The difference is that the message you send isn't e-mailed to everyone on a list. Instead, it's stored on a news server, which in turn copies the message to other news servers. When you want to read a message on the newsgroup, you use a news reader program that connects you to a news server. To read newsgroups in this manner, your Internet service provider must receive a news feed, and you must configure your newsreader to pick up the feed.

Don't worry if you don't have access to a news feed through your Internet service provider. Some sites — such as DejaNews (www.deja.com) — enable you to view and post to newsgroups over the World Wide Web.

You can also receive posts from newsgroups through gatewayed mailing lists. *Gatewayed* means that traffic from newsgroups is relayed to a mailing list and vice versa. You can find a list of the gatewayed newsgroups in the Genealogy Resources on the Internet Web site at members.aol.com/gfsjohnf/gen_mail.html.

Posting protocol

All newsgroups have *charters* that define the scope of the newsgroup. Some newsgroup *moderators* (people who help manage the newsgroup) frequently post the charters and tips on using newsgroups. If you can't find the group's charter, the safest thing to do is see what other people post before you post yourself. You can also consult the Usenet Newsgroup Charter Archive at www.faqs.org/usenet/gsearch.html.

The soc.genealogy.surnames groups are moderated, which means that you can't post directly to them. When you send a message to a moderated newsgroup, it's first reviewed by an *automoderator*, a computer program that determines which of the surnames groups your message is posted in. Because a computer screens your message, formatting is very critical. The subject line of all queries requires a certain format, which you can find in the Frequently Asked Questions (FAQ) files located at www.rootsweb.com/~surnames/. Here are a few examples of acceptable subject lines:

```
Subject: HELM George / Dorothea; Frederick Co.,
VA,USA; 1723-1769
Subject: HELM; VA,USA > TN,USA > IL,USA; 1723-
Subject: HELM; VA,USA>TN,USA>IL,USA; 1723-
Subject: HELM; anywhere; anytime
Subject: HELM Web Page; ENG / USA; 1723-
```

Be sure to include the correct abbreviations for the locations in your subject line. These codes determine which newsgroups the automoderator places your message in. You can find a list of the acceptable location codes on the Roots Surname List Country Abbreviations page (www.rootsweb.com roots-l/cabbrev1.html). Also, be sure to place an e-mail address at the end of your query so that interested researchers can contact you directly.

WARNING!

Don't believe everything you read!

No matter what sort of research you're doing, always verify any information that you find online. If you can't verify the information with some authoritative record, then the information simply may not be worth anything. However, just because you can't immediately prove this tidbit doesn't mean that you shouldn't hold on to the information. At some time in the future, you may run across a record that does indeed prove the accuracy of the information.

Finding Family Reunions

Family reunions enable you to visit relatives you haven't seen in a long time and to meet new relatives you may never have known otherwise! Reunions are a wonderful opportunity to build your genealogical base by chatting with relatives about old family stories, ancestors, and the like.

Although a reunion doesn't feel like a formal interview, it can give you much of the same information as if you sat down and formally interviewed each of the people in attendance. Taking along a tape recorder or video camera is a good idea because you don't have to worry about writing down everything your relatives say right at that moment — you can just sit back and enjoy talking with your family. Plus, your genealogy is greatly enhanced by audio or video tape. (Just make sure that when you're going to tape a conversation, you have the permission of those relatives you plan to record.)

Family reunions also offer you the opportunity to share what you know about the family and exchange genealogical records and reports. If you know ahead of time that several of your relatives are also into genealogical research, you can better plan with them what records, pictures, reports, and other resources to bring. Remember, your work doesn't have to be complete or perfect in grammar for others to enjoy seeing what you've collected.

To find out about family reunions, watch the family association and one-name study Web sites of the surnames that you're researching. Typically, these types of Web pages have sections set up for reunion announcements. Also, see the *Reunions Magazine* site (www.reunionsmag.com).

Sharing Pictures Electronically

Being able to send digital photos to friends and family around the world via e-mail is one of the more enjoyable aspects of owning a computer. With a few clicks of your mouse, you can send an image to anyone who has an e-mail account. That person can then view your image on-screen, save it to disk, and even edit and print it.

Although attaching an image to an e-mail message is really simple, the process sometimes breaks down due to differences in e-mail programs and how files are handled on the Mac versus the PC. Also, newcomers to the world of electronic mail often get confused about how to view and send images — which isn't surprising, given that e-mail software often makes the process less than intuitive.

One way to help make sure that your image arrives intact is to prepare it properly before sending:

- ✔ Size your image to a 640-x-480 display.

- ✔ Save your image in the JPEG format. (If you're sending an image to a CompuServe user, then you may have to save your image in GIF format instead — if one format doesn't work, use the other.)

  Note: These instructions don't apply to images that you're sending to someone who needs the image for some professional graphics purpose — for example, if you created an image for your company newsletter. In that case, save the image file in whatever format you're told to, and use the image resolution appropriate for the final output.

With large image files, expect long download times. As a matter of fact, unless you're on a tight deadline, putting the image on a Zip disk or some other removable storage medium and sending it off via overnight mail may be a better option than e-mail transmission.

Dealing with special circumstances

If the image doesn't arrive as expected or can't be viewed, the first thing to do is call the tech support line for the recipient's e-mail program or service. Find out whether you need to follow any special procedures when sending images and verify that the recipient's software is set up correctly. If everything seems okay on that end, contact your own e-mail provider or software tech support. Chances are some e-mail setting needs to be tweaked, and the tech support personnel should be able to help you resolve the problem quickly.

For special images, you may want to send an e-mail "postcard" instead of attaching your file to a standard e-mail message. With a postcard, your recipient sees your message and image laid out in a design that resembles a traditional postcard. In some cases, you can even add an audio message. Following are two options for sending postcards:

✔ Kodak offers a free postcard service at its Web site (click the Picture This Postcards link on the home page, www.kodak.com); you upload your picture to the site, add a message, and enter the recipient's e-mail address. The recipient then goes to the Kodak site to view the postcard.

✔ You can also buy postcard software programs to design your own. With these programs, you attach your post-card file to an e-mail message along with a viewer that enables the recipient to view your handiwork. Or you can convert the postcard to a standard JPEG file so a viewer isn't necessary.

Compiling electronic photo albums

After you get all those images onto your hard drive, Zip disk, or other image warehouse, you need to organize them so that you can easily find a particular image.

If you're a no-frills type of person, you can simply organize your images into folders, as you do your word-processing files, spreadsheets, and other documents. You may want to keep all images shot during a particular year or month in one folder, with images segregated into subfolders by subject. For example, your main folder may be named 2000, and your subfolders may be named Family, Sunsets, Holidays, Work, and so on.

Many image editors include a utility that enables you to browse through your image folders and view *thumbnails* (a tiny version of the original) of each image. These utilities allow you to easily track down a particular image if you can't quite remember what you named the thing.

You can also buy stand-alone viewer utilities, such as ThumbsPlus, a shareware program from Cerious Software. This particular viewer enables you to see your images in several different layouts, including one that mimics the Windows Explorer format, as shown in Figure 3-2. To organize images, you can drag and drop them from one folder to another. You can also perform some limited image editing in this program.

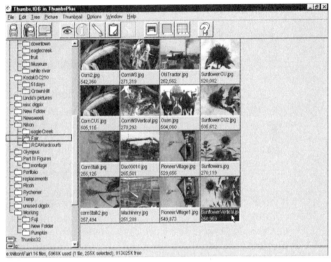

Figure 3-2: ThumbsPlus is a shareware program that enables you to view your images by using a Windows Explorer-style interface.

If you want a fancier setup, several programs enable you to organize and view your images using an old-fashioned photo-album motif. Figure 3-3 offers a look at one such program, Presto! PhotoAlbum, from NewSoft. You drag images from a browser onto album pages, where you can then label the images and record information, such as the date and place the image was shot. You can also place your images inside frames and add other special on-screen touches.

Photo-album programs are great for those times when you want to leisurely review your images or show them to others — much as you would enjoy a traditional photo album. And creating a digital photo album can be a fun project to enjoy with your kids — they'll love picking out frames for images and adding other special effects.

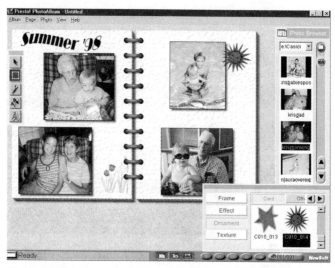

Figure 3-3: Programs such as Presto! PhotoAlbum enable you to organize your pictures by using a traditional photo-album motif.

If your image collection is large, you may want to look for a catalog program that enables you to store reference data with each image, such as a category, description, and the date the picture was taken. Some programs also enable you to list a few keywords with each image that can make hunting down the image easier in the future. For example, if you have an image of a Labrador retriever, you may enter the keywords "dog," "retriever," and "pet." When you later run the search portion of the browser, entering any of those keywords as a search criteria brings up the image. These kinds of tools can be extremely helpful when you start to accumulate large quantities of images. ThumbsPlus and PhotoRecall are among the programs offering this feature.

Part II
Things to Do

REVEREND DAVIS PAUSES DURING HIS SERMON TO BID ON A DUKES OF HAZZARD SMOKIN' GENERAL LEE SNOWBOARD.

In this part . . .

*I*f you're traveling, you need something that assures you you're heading in the right direction. You don't want to drive 50 miles out of your way with two bored children in tow. You also need to know what to wear. No use packing shorts for your trip to Disney World if Florida is having a cold snap. Finally, you need to know what you're going to do when you get to your destination. No need to wait three hours to get seated at a restaurant only to find that the locals go to a little bistro three blocks over. This part shows you where to find maps, weather information, and city guides.

If you're vacation-ready but savings-poor, you may want to consider selling some of the things you no longer need through an online auction. You'll find that information in this part, too.

Chapter 4

Reading the Signs in Your City and Beyond

● ●

● ●

*T*he hardest part of packing for a vaction is guessing what to pack based on what the weather may — or may not — do. The most intimidating thing about visiting a city for the first time is figuring out where to eat, what to do, and what areas may be dangerous. This chapter tells you how to use the Internet to scout out your destination and the local weather before you set foot out your front door. And, who knows — you may even discover some of your own town's best-kept secrets along the way.

Getting Under the Weather

On the one hand, life would be pretty boring without storms and wind; but on the other hand, traveling in bad weather is no fun (and sometimes dangerous). Whether you're a leisure traveler, frequent business traveler, or an amateur meteorologist, you can make your travels much smoother by planning for the weather by using the Internet.

The weather technology available on the Internet allows skiers to get the current snow conditions and cruisers to check the status of tropical storms. If you're driving somewhere, you can log on to the Internet to find out whether the roadways are flooded. Or maybe you just want know what to wear outside. The best weather Web sites provide a wide range of advanced weather technology, including the following features:

- ✔ Current weather and conditions for numerous locales
- ✔ Extended forecasts
- ✔ Satellite imagery
- ✔ A variety of weather radar maps
- ✔ Customization ability
- ✔ Special weather features, historical data, and news reports

Mapping and weather sites are necessarily heavy on graphics. If you have a slow connection, prepare for longer downloads on some sites.

You don't have to look too far on the Web to find tons of weather info. Check out the Yahoo! weather category listing (www.yahoo.com/news_and_media/weather) and you find a mind-boggling number of listings. Thank goodness that you don't have to plow through all of these sites to find the good ones — we've done all that for you.

AccuWeather

AccuWeather (www.accuweather.com), Figure 4-1, has been a leader in the field of weather forecasting for many years; many professional news services use AccuWeather data to prepare their own weather reports.

To get a quick check of the weather in a specific city, enter the city's zip code or name into the box under the heading Enter Your Local City on the home page. For U.S. weather forecasts, AccuWeather presents you with a look at the current conditions by way of three satellite radar maps (national Doppler radar, local Doppler, and a satellite map of the cloud cover). AccuWeather also shows you a five-day forecast for the city with high and low temperatures for each day.

Figure 4-1: Professional weathercasters use the AccuWeather home page.

For worldwide five day forecasts, click World in the left-hand navigation bar. You can then select a country and a city from the menus that represent the different continents of the world. You can also click one of the world regions under World Satellite Features for satellite views of the cloud cover.

Sun worshippers will appreciate the Recreation Weather section at AccuWeather. Clicking the Recreation Weather button (on the left navigation bar) brings you to a page where you can choose to view either the Beach and Boating Forecast or the Ray Ban UV Index. Beach and Boating, as you may guess, gives the coastal weather conditions for 44 regions of the U.S., complete with tanning index and wave heights. The Ray Ban UV Index uses a map of the U.S. to show where the ultraviolet light levels are the highest and most dangerous each day.

AccuWeather also allows you to create a personalized weather page that you can set to automatically look up the weather in the area you want to know about. The service has a subscription fee; you can have a free 30 day trial, but after the trial, you must pay a monthly fee, according to a sliding scale. For personal use, it costs $4.95 per month. For educational or corporate use, the fees are a bit higher.

Intellicast

The clean design at Intellicast (www.intellicast.com), Figure 4-2, makes finding the weather in your neighborhood or across the globe an easy task.

Figure 4-2: The Intellicast home page has a clean design.

You can use either the links on the left side of the page or on the top to navigate through the various sections of the site, which include the following:

- ✔ **USA Weather:** Maps and forecasts for the U.S.

- ✔ **World Weather:** Worldwide maps and forecasts

- ✔ **Travel:** Forecasts geared towards travelers

- ✔ **Ski Reports:** Snow conditions at resorts around the world

- ✔ **Health:** Reports on the impact of weather on your health

- ✔ **Almanac:** Facts and statistics from the world of meteorology

For weather information about cities in the U.S., click USA Weather to access a map of the U.S. Click the appropriate city, or if the city you want to check didn't make the map, use the list of links below the map to locate your city or region. A city's weather listing on Intellicast gives the four-day forecast as well as the expected high and low temperatures. To see the various satellite maps and radar views (like you see on the evening newscasts), click the links on the left side of the page. You can choose from the following views:

> ✔ **Radar:** Use Radar to see precipitation and storm action.
>
> ✔ **Radar Loop:** A composite of several radar images, taken at timed intervals, looped together. Use this map to watch the progress of a storm.
>
> Radar Loop is a cool feature but beware — loading each image takes time, and the loop doesn't run until all the images are loaded.
>
> ✔ **Radar Summary:** A type of radar that provides detailed storm info.
>
> ✔ **NEXRAD:** An advanced radar system that shows weather events with more accuracy than other radar systems.
>
> ✔ **Satellite and Satellite Loop:** The satellite image is taken by a satellite orbiting the Earth and allows you to see actual photos of clouds and storm systems. The Satellite Loop is similar to the Radar Loop, but with satellite images instead of radar scans.

Unfortunately, these maps are only available for the U.S. For the rest of the world, Intellicast has four-day forecasts and satellite images for your weather viewing pleasure.

For a look at current weather conditions and forecasts for other places in the world, click World (duh!) and select the region or city you wish to know about. If your inner Celsius to Fahrenheit converter isn't all it should be, use the one provided by the site (on the left navigation bar) to translate the scale into a recognizable number.

The Travel section at Intellicast quickly shows you the weather in dozens of cities in the U.S.; click the city name to see a more detailed report. If you and the family are heading out to the U.S. National Parks, make sure that you stop in at the section specifically for parks' forecasts. In addition, the site offers a section devoted to golfers, skiers, and sailors to address the specific weather-related needs of those who putt, schuss, and tack.

Finally, Intellicast features Dr. Dewpoint, an expert meteorologist, who discusses the day's most compelling weather stories in detail.

Mapping Out a Plan

Even if you consider yourself to have a good sense of direction, online mapping sites can help you plan a road trip, aiding you in getting from point A to point B without a blow to your ego. Or, if you simply have a love of maps, you'll enjoy playing with these fun and easy-to-use sites. These sites offer additional features that travelers will appreciate: Mapping sites are equally adept at generating maps and driving instructions.

The following three sites have proven themselves to be the best bets when you're in need of a map:

- DeLorme's CyberRouter
  (www.delorme.com/CyberMaps/route.asp)
- MapQuest (www.mapquest.com)
- Maps On Us (www.mapsonus.com)

Each of the preceding sites can draw you a map of any place in the U. S. and provide driving directions if you enter a starting and destination point. The map quality is fairly equal on each. MapQuest and Maps On Us differentiate themselves by allowing you to enter exact starting and destination points for driving instructions (door to door), while DeLorme's CyberRouter only creates city-to-city directions. Using these mapping sites is easy, and the process is very similar on each.

Using Online City Guides

A new and unfamiliar city can be one of the most daunting places to navigate for a just-arriving traveler. Unless you have a friend or relative living in each city you visit, you're dependent on your wits and a city guide for all the decisions you make. The city guides you find on the Internet can save you from buying three or four different (heavy) books about your destination; but the Internet won't save you from visiting your Aunt Carol and Uncle Peter if they've promised to "show you the town."

A quality online city guide directs you to all a city has to offer, including the following:

- ✔ Places to eat
- ✔ Sights to see
- ✔ Nightlife options
- ✔ Movie timetables
- ✔ Sporting events
- ✔ Art galleries and exhibitions, festivals, and theater performances
- ✔ Neighborhoods to check out (and those to avoid)

Online city guides provide a terrific alternative to the singular voice of the guidebook. But the most important advantage an online city guide offers over a conventional, print guide is that online information gets updated all the time. The city information you find on the Web is often the most current available. Try finding a movie timetable in a print guidebook!

The Web houses dozens — in many cases hundreds — of guides for every city on the big blue marble of planet Earth.

Several major commercial efforts for city guides are currently establishing themselves in cities across the U.S. and in other countries. These city guide networks generally maintain staffs comprised of local editors, critics, and writers in each selected city, offering first-hand knowledge of the city in a standardized format. This way, if you're familiar with one city's guide, you won't have to figure out a whole new system to read another city guide that's part of the same network.

The major city guide networks all have some serious investment behind them (for example, Microsoft backs the Sidewalk guides, which you can read more about later in this chapter). Creating and maintaining up-to-date, comprehensive, and accurate information about a place as big as say, New York City, is extremely expensive. For almost every city, there exist small, non-commercial sites that are maintained by people who are passionate about their hometown, or the city in which they reside. But a big, commercial city guide undoubtedly out-performs a guide produced by one dude in his basement when he gets home from his 9-to-5 each day.

The following sections detail the many features of the four biggest online city guide networks, allowing you to get a feel for their many features.

CitySearch

CitySearch (www.citysearch.com), Figure 4-3, publishes guides for several cities worldwide, most of which are in the U.S. (including New York, Los Angeles, and Washington and also smaller cities such as Nashville and Austin). City search also currently offers guides to Melbourne and Sydney, Australia and Toronto, Canada. To access any city's guide, click the appropriate place on the map.

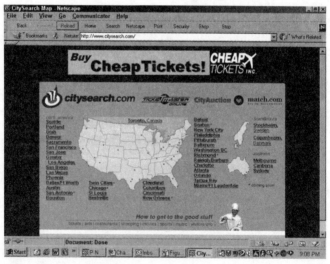

Figure 4-3: The CitySearch home page is always adding new city guides.

CitySearch provides a good deal of editorial advice, meaning it doesn't just tell you a club's address and give you no details to go on. For most of its listings, editors visit the place they're writing about and then relay the ambiance, the prices, the type of people who go there, and other relevant information to you. CitySearch also makes excellent use of photography to illustrate the restaurants and venues it reviews.

Getting around each site is a fairly simple affair. Use the category links (Arts & Entertainment, Eat & Drink, Community, Sports & Outdoors, and so on) on the left hand side of each guide to move through the sections that interest you.

Each page of each CitySearch guide has a search box in the upper-left-hand corner labeled, "What Are You Looking For?" Use the search box at any time to quickly perform a search for anything and everything.

Each CitySearch guide features a section specifically for visitors to its city. This section contains editors' picks for special events, activities, or sights that may be of particular interest to a visitor.

Digital City

Digital City (www.digitalcity.com) currently covers more than 36 American cities on its WebGuides (including New York, Los Angeles, New Orleans, Chicago, Cleveland, and Chapel Hill) and the same 36 (or so) cities on America Online. Digital City is owned by America Online, so they have many resources to produce complete guides.

These guides generally act as comprehensive Yellow Pages-type directories, with varying degrees of editorial content. Click the map of the U.S. to access a guide for the city you're traveling to.

For each city, you find what you're looking for by going to the category of your interest. Looking for a restaurant in Denver? Click Restaurants in the Entertainment section (restaurants are *so* entertaining) and you're presented with a list of links to online restaurant directories for Denver and some links to actual restaurants' Web pages.

Digital City guides have varying degrees of editorial content (restaurant reviews, movie critiques, and so on); bigger cities tend to have more in-depth guides. Some of Digital City's guides offer unique, first-hand reviews of the features they cover; other guides are made up of only collections of links to other sites' directories. In New York's guide, for example, the writers review restaurants, bars, and all the other stuff critics critique, while Denver's guide is mostly composed of reviewed Web sites. (This discrepancy is probably dictated by what the other online guides in the city are offering.) All in all, Digital City WebGuides are not as authoritative and useful as city guides that consistently write their own reviews.

Sidewalk

The Sidewalk city guides (www.sidewalk.com), sponsored by Microsoft, offer insight into all aspects of a city's life through painstaking reporting and well-crafted reviews. Click the name of a city on the Sidewalk home page to access a specific guide.

Microsoft prides itself on its ability to create well-designed software that has a high level of functionality. The Sidewalk guides are no exception. You can access all the information you need on Sidewalk by using any of the following methods:

- **Using the Fast Finder:** If you know what you're looking for, type an appropriate keyword into the Fast Finder (the search box on each guide's home page) and away you go.

- **Browsing:** Using the horizontal navigation bar at the top of each guide page, click the links to Movies, Restaurants, Arts & Events, Places, Sports, and Traffic View to peruse the offerings.

- **Searching:** Each Sidewalk guide offers a series of links that guide you through a search. Click Find a Movie, Find an Event, or Find a Restaurant to use the clever system of search boxes that search by neighborhood, price range, and other criteria.

  For example, say that you want to search for a restaurant. Click Find a Restaurant (on any guide). Using the five pull-down menus, select a neighborhood, a cuisine, a price range, and a star rating. (Each variable is optional. If you just want to search in a specific neighborhood, select only a neighborhood.) When you're ready, click the Go! button and the site presents you with a list of restaurants that match your specifications.

One of the coolest things about Sidewalk is its ability to let you customize the site, making it easy to find the things that interest you. Customizing the offerings takes some effort, but if you plan on visiting a city often, you should spend the time.

After you select all your choices, the site asks you to enter your favorite performers or events into the Personal Agent. When your choices are coming to town, Sidewalk sends you an e-mail notification. (Can't wait for that e-mail!)

The site displays your picks at the bottom of the home page. Each time you visit, the site updates the information. You can update your choices at any time by selecting Change Custom Options.

TimeOut

The TimeOut guides (www.timeout.com), Figure 4-4, are the most global of the major city guide networks, currently operating in 29 cities worldwide, including Amsterdam, Barcelona, Las Vegas, Miami, Prague, and Tokyo.

Figure 4-4: TimeOut is your entry into city guides across the globe.

TimeOut (both in print and online), is targeted towards a young, trendy, urban audience and the tone of the writing is best described as hip and in-the-know. Though it may not be as in-depth as CitySearch and Sidewalk, TimeOut's online guides complement its well-known print versions in many of the featured cities, drawing on the pithy content from those publications.

The most valuable section of each online TimeOut guide is the Events section, which lists the goings on for the next two weeks. The site organizes the listings by categories, which include Art, Children, Clubs, Comedy, Dance, Film, Music, Sports, and Theatre.

You may also want to check out the City Guide section that contains "detailed, critical listings on accommodations, sight-seeing, arts, entertainment, and eating and drinking in the city." We couldn't say it better ourselves.

Small, independent online guides

The large, commercial city guides have one major downside; they're large and commercial. Sometimes they feel a little stilted — kind of like your mother trying to tell you what's cool. For example, say you're headed to San Francisco to make a business contact and relax for a few days. Aside from a short stint on the Haight in 1969, you haven't a clue what's going on in the city by the Bay. But you're still hip and want to find some good nightlife. San Francisco Sidewalk (`sanfrancisco.sidewalk.com`) offers some insight, but seems a bit sterile.

Instead of missing out, do a search on one of the search engines to find some less commercial city guides. Virtually every city has a host of guides maintained by local people, some are for profit (they sell ads) and others are created just for the fun of it.

Using city guides that aren't part of huge, multimillion-dollar initiatives has the following advantages:

> ✓ **A small guide may have an opinionated, local view-point:** Only someone who hangs out regularly in a club really knows what the scene is like. Critics from a commercial guide probably visit only once. The same holds true for restaurants and other venues; locally produced guides are full of insider advice.

✔ **A small guide can cater to a specific type of traveler:** A guide produced by a young Web aficionado speaks to young people better than a guide produced by a middle-aged baby-boomer.

✔ **Many small guides have no annoying advertising:** Because commercial guides depend on advertising dollars to pay the bills, they often inundate you with all sorts of ads. Small, local guides are generally produced just for love and won't annoy you with pop-up ads.

✔ **Small guides have the ability to cover more off-beat topics:** Guides come in all shapes and sizes. Some guides just talk about bars. Some just talk about restaurants. Some just talk. It's all up to the person creating the guide.

Because the smaller city guides don't generally have an advertising budget, you're probably not going to have their names on the tip of your tongue. Yahoo! (www.yahoo.com), the ubiquitous Web directory, provides one of the best tools for locating the wide range of city guides. You can either enter your search words directly into the search box (San Francisco guide, for example) or click the Travel heading to drill down through Yahoo's directories.

Looking for Festivals and Events Online

Sightseeing is fun. But sometimes you want to go beyond just looking around. Before your next trip, consult one of the many festivals and events databases on the World Wide Web. Whether you're looking for an outdoor concert in Golden Gate Park or the Australian Film Festival, the Internet is the perfect medium for finding interesting stuff to do at your destinations.

Festivals.com

Festivals.com (www.festivals.com), Figure 4-5, is the premier festivals and events database on the Web. The site lets you search for events at your destination. For example, say you're going on a trip to Quebec for a long weekend in Montreal.

Here's how you would go about using Festivals.com to find some fun and interesting events in the area:

1. **Click the map of the world to enter the Festival Finder.**

2. **You can then use either the map of the world (click Canada, then Quebec) or type** Montreal **and a date into the search box.**

   The database displays the events for the coming months in the province of Quebec, many of which are located in Montreal. If the festival or event has a Web site of its own, you can click the name of the event to visit the page.

Figure 4-5: Festivals.com highlights events in cities you may be visiting.

Festivals.com also has some other helpful resources. You can read the latest on noteworthy events or find a book about an event's subject. The site also provides, for your clicking pleasure, a list of online travelers' resources on the Travel Assistance page.

(Festivals.com is a trademark of RSL Interactive, Inc. All contents on Festivals.com are copyrighted property of RSL Interactive, Inc., Pier 55, Suite 288, 1101 Alaskan Way, Seattle, WA, 98101.)

CultureFinder

Does your idea of culture contain less county fair and more ballet? Then CultureFinder (www.culturefinder.com), Figure 4-6, is the site for you. Billing itself as the "online address for the arts," CultureFinder maintains a database of dance recitals, theater events, gallery openings, ballet recitals, and more. The listings cover over 550 cities in the United States and several European cities.

Figure 4-6: CultureFinder helps you find theater, opera, dance, and more.

Begin your search by using the Calendar. Tell CultureFinder what type of event you're looking for and when it should be happening. You can also search by many other ways, such as geographic location, venue, organization, and so on. Or use the pull-down menu to select a city's entire culture calendar.

Also, if you're headed to Boston, Chicago, Los Angeles, New York, Philadelphia, San Francisco, St. Louis, or Washington D.C., CultureFinder has a complete city guide to aid you in your cultural expedition. Go to CityGuides and select your city of interest. These guides list the current week's happenings (cultural events are broken down by category), complete with phone numbers and addresses to venues.

Chapter 5

Cleaning Out and Cleaning Up

· ·

· ·

*A*uctions, exciting though they may be, can be very intimidating. Surely you've seen a movie or TV show where someone ends up bidding an astronomical amount for an ugly green vase because he shooed a fly away at just the wrong moment. That scenario isn't a worry in the online auction world. This chapter gives you the scoop on wheeling and dealing on the Web. If you're buying, read on for the sites to see. If you're selling, read the ins and outs of online sales, including using pictures to generate more profit.

Going, Going, Gone All Into Auctions

An *auction* is a unique sales event where the exact value of the item for sale is unknown, resulting in an element of surprise not only for the bidder (who may end up with a great deal), but for the seller (who may end up making a killing). A seller fills out an electronic form and sets the auction up, listing a *minimum bid* he or she is willing to accept for the item.

Bidders duke it out over a period of time (sometimes three days, but usually a week or even longer) until one comes out victorious. Usually, the highest bidder wins.

eBay, one of the most popular online auction sites, offers five types of auctions — as do most other auction sites:

- ✔ **Traditional auctions:** Did you ever hear those motor-mouthed auctioneers raising the price of an item until they say "going once, going twice, sold?" They're conducting *traditional* auctions, and the majority of items sold on eBay (one of the most popular online auction sites) are sold this way. Traditional auctions are simple: The highest bidder takes home the prize.

- ✔ **Reserve-price auctions:** A *reserve price* protects a seller from having to sell an item for less than it's actually worth. The reserve price allows sellers to set lower minimum bids, and lower minimum bids attract bidders. Unfortunately, if a seller makes the reserve price too high and it isn't met by the end of the auction, no one wins. Nobody — except the seller and the auction site's computer system — knows what the reserve price is until the auction is over, but you can tell from the auction page whether you're dealing with a reserve-price auction. If anyone has bid on an item, a message also appears on the page saying whether the reserve price has been met. (***Note:*** eBay does charge a fee for sellers to run these auctions.)

- ✔ **Restricted-access auctions:** If you're over 18 years of age and interested in bidding on items of an adult nature, eBay has an Adults Only category, which has restricted access. Although you can peruse the other eBay categories without having to hand over credit card information, you must have a credit card number on file with eBay to view and bid on items in this category. Restricted-access auctions are run the same as every other eBay auction.

If you're worried that your children may be able to gain access to graphic adult material, eBay's solved that problem by excluding adult-content items from easily accessible areas. Besides, children under the age of 18 aren't allowed to register for eBay and should be under an adult's supervision if they do wander onto the site.

If you're interested in bidding on adult merchandise, remember that legal statutes regulate the sale and distribution of adult materials. In other words, know the laws where you live.

✔ **Private (mind-your-own-business) auctions:** Private auctions are run like traditional auctions except that each bidder's identity is kept secret. At the end of the auction, eBay provides contact info to the seller and to the high bidder, and that's it. You can send e-mail questions to the seller in a private auction, but you can't check out your competition because the auction item page shows the current bid price, but not the high bidder's User ID.

✔ **Dutch auctions:** A *Dutch auction* allows a seller to put multiple, identical items up for sale. As a buyer, you *can* elect to bid on any number from one to the whole lot. You can't conduct a Dutch auction as a private auction.

eBaying Away

eBay (www.ebay.com), shown in Figure 5-1, is the best-known and most successful online auction site, receiving hundreds of thousands of bids each day. You can find anything, new or used, including more unusual items such as tickets to events. eBay features inexpensive, moderate, and big ticket items. It provides a history for every buyer and seller, as well as auction insurance. If you're an extrovert, you can chat with other customers and auctioneers; if you're an introvert, you can read the eBay newsletter. This site is the home of Rosie O'Donnell's much publicized charity auctions.

You gain big-time rewards for selling on eBay by

✔ Starting a business for little or no money.

✔ Getting a taste of running a business.

✔ Clearing out your household clutter.

✔ Making as much money as you are willing to work for.

✔ Learning about your items while selling.

✔ Teaching your kids life lessons.

✔ Having fun wheeling and dealing.

Figure 5-1: The eBay Home page is your gateway to almost any product you can imagine.

Most people starting a business have to worry about rounding up *investment capital* (start-up money they may lose), building inventory (buying stuff to sell), and finding a selling location like a booth at a swap meet or even a small store. Today, even a little Mom-and-Pop start-up operation requires a major investment. eBay's helped to level the playing field a bit; everybody gets an equal chance to start a small business with just a little money. Anyone who wants to take a stab at doing business can get started with just enough money to cover the Insertion Fee (see the section "eBay's fees" later in this chapter).

Start your budding business empire with just one item. Put the item up for auction, get it sold, collect the payment, and ship it out. Or, to paraphrase instructions from shampoo bottles, "Sell, ship, repeat."

Get a few transactions under your belt. See how you like the responsibilities of marketing, collecting money, shipping, and customer service.

eBay's no-no's and maybe nots

Officially, the biggest no-no's on eBay are

- Items that are prohibited from being bought, sold, or owned in the state of California
- Items that infringe on a third party's ownership of a trademark, copyright, logo, or any other form of intellectual property
- Any item for which eBay can be liable

The items that you absolutely *cannot* sell on eBay fit into *all three* categories. Those items can be legally ambiguous at best, not to mention potentially risky and all kinds of sticky. Because eBay's base of operations is in California, United States law is enforced — even if both buyer and seller are from other countries. Although possessing (and selling) many of the items in the following list is legal in the United States and elsewhere, you are absolutely, positively *prohibited* from buying and selling the following on eBay:

- Firearms of all types
- Military weapons
- Police and other law enforcement badges and IDs (or copies or reproductions of them)
- Pets and wildlife, including animal parts from endangered species
- Child pornography
- Forged items
- Items that infringe on someone else's copyright or trademark
- Stolen items

But take heart, media buffs — here are some promotional items that you probably can sell on eBay:

- Movie press kits
- Clothing, as long as the item isn't counterfeit
- Gifts

Certifying the real McCoy

If you're in the market for an autograph, don't even consider bidding on one unless it comes with a *Certificate of Authenticity* (COA). Reputable sellers offer COAs as a means of ensuring that what you see is exactly what you get. Many sellers take authenticity so seriously that they give buyers the right to a full refund if any doubt about authenticity crops up.

Don't assume that just because an item has a COA that the item is authentic. Unfortunately, COAs can be forged, too. Be sure to check the authenticity of the authenticator; a good place to start is the feedback area. If they have many happy customers, you may be okay.

Intellectual property owners actively defend their rights and, along with the help from average eBay users, continually tip eBay off to fraudulent and infringing auctions. Rights owners can use eBay's Verified Rights Owner (VeRO) program, as well as law-enforcement agencies.

eBay's verboten auctions

The folks at eBay didn't just fall off the turnip truck. eBay staffers have seen just about every scam to get around paying fees or following policy guidelines. Chances are good that if you try one of these, you'll get caught. eBay cancels the auction and credits you for the listing fee. Do it once, shame on you! Do it often and you're out of eBay!

- ✔ **Raffles and prizes:** You need to *sell* something in your auction, not offer tickets or chances for a giveaway.

- ✔ **Want ads:** If you want something, make a posting on the Wanted Board — don't try to pass an ad off as an auction.

- ✔ **Advertisements:** An eBay auction is not the place to make a sales pitch for some other auction or Web site.

- ✔ **Bait-and-switch:** A variation on the ugly old sales technique of pretending to sell what you're not really selling.

✔ **Choice auctions:** Offering a mishmash of multiple items, choice auctions don't work because bidders don't really know what they've bought until the auction is over.

✔ **Mixing apples with oranges:** This gambit tries to attract more bidders to view an item by putting it in a high-traffic category where it doesn't belong.

✔ **Catalogues:** "Buy my catalogue so you buy more stuff from me!" In a word, nope.

eBay's fees

On eBay you don't have to spend *much* to run your business. With over 250,000 items going up for auction every day, eBay makes their money in volume. eBay charges three types of fees for conducting auctions:

✔ Insertion Fees (from $.25 to $2.00)

✔ Final Value Fees (a percentage of the sales price)

✔ Optional Fees (which vary)

Window Shopping at Other Auction Sites

eBay may be the best-known auction site, but it's certainly not the only one out there. The following list gives you a smattering of other online auction sites that may interest you:

✔ **Amazon.com Auctions** (www.amazon.com): Amazon now offers a huge auction in many categories, from baseballs to books. This auction is worth checking out just because of the number of people who are buying and selling.

✔ **AuctionAddict.com** (www.auctionaddict.com): AuctionAddict.com features person–to-person auctions (and therefore doesn't act as a broker and doesn't guarantee prices or goods) and a classified ad venue with no listing fees. Users are billed monthly.

✔ **Auction Universe** (www.auctionuniverse.com): Whether you want to buy or sell a single item or are a passionate collector of just about everything, you'll find what you're looking for here.

✔ **Keybuy Auction House** (www.keybuy.com): This auction has no commission and no listing fees, making it one of the only completely free auctions on the Internet. This may change, however, so keep your eyes peeled for new charges.

✔ **OpenIPO** (www.openipo.com): Bid for stock on this site. In OpenIPO auctions, unlike other auctions, bidding is completely secret, and the winning bidders all pay the same price of the lowest winning bid.

✔ **The Sharper Image** (auction.sharperimage.com/osauction.shtml): This site auctions Shaper Image goods — ranging from jukeboxes to shoe fresheners — that are brand new, repackaged, refurbished, and/or one-of-a-kind items.

✔ **Sotheby's** (www.sothebys.com): Offering links to live auctions, free catalogs, a calendar of events, and collecting searches, this site is a good one for the international, exotic collector.

✔ **uAuction** (www.uauction.com/index.html): uAuction features auctions of antiques, collectibles, sports memorabilia, dolls, books (first edition and new fiction), cars (classic to new parts and tools), computer hardware, general merchandise, music, pet accessories, sports, stamps, and jewelry (vintage and new).

✔ **Yahoo! Auctions** (auctions.yahoo.com): Providing links to hundreds of online auctions that specialize in virtually everything, this site is a great place to start your search for a specific item.

Using Images in Your Auctions

Would you buy an item you couldn't see first? Most people wouldn't, especially if they're interested in purchasing collectible items that they want to display. Without a picture, you can't tell whether a seller's idea of "good quality" is anything like yours. With the advent of digital cameras and scanners, you can add *images* (cyper-speak for pictures) of what you're selling to your auction page.

You can easily place images from your digital camera onto your Web pages. This section provides some how-to advice on a general artistic and technical level.

Choosing a digital camera

If price isn't a factor, buy the highest-quality digital camera you can afford, especially if you plan to use images with many of your online auctions, and the items you plan to sell vary in size and shape. eBay — surprise! — is a great place to buy digital cameras. Just do a search of some popular manufacturers like Olympus, Fujifilm, Sony, and Nikon, and you will find pages of auction listings for both new and used digital cameras.

Whether you buy new or used digital equipment on eBay, make sure that it comes with a warranty. If you *don't* get a warranty, Murphy's Law practically guarantees that your digital equipment will break the second time you use it.

Look for the following features:

- ✓ **Resolution:** Look for a camera that has a resolution of at least 640 x 480 pixels.

- ✓ **Storage type:** The instructions with your camera explain how to transfer images to your computer.

- ✓ **Extra features:** Make sure that the camera is capable of taking close-up images. (A flash also comes in handy.) If you plan to sell small or detailed items that require extreme close-ups — stamps or coins, for example — look for a digital camera that lets you change lenses.

Composing your pictures

Not everyone agrees on the "best" ways to compose an image — art being in the eye of the beholder and all that. For every composition rule, you can find an incredible image that proves the exception. That said, the following list offers some suggestions that can help you create images that rise above the ho-hum mark on the visual interest meter:

- ✔ **Remember the rule of thirds:** For maximum impact, don't place your subject smack in the center of the frame. Instead, mentally divide the image area into thirds, as Figure 5-2 illustrates. Then position the main subject elements at spots where the dividing lines intersect.

- ✔ **Draw the eye across the frame:** To add life to your images, compose the scene so that the viewer's eye is naturally drawn from one edge of the frame to the other, as in Figure 5-3.

- ✔ **Avoid the plant-on-the-head syndrome:** In other words, watch out for distracting background elements.

- ✔ **Shoot your subject from unexpected angles:** Don't be afraid to climb up on a chair (a sturdy chair, of course) or lie on the ground to catch your subject from a unique point of view.

- ✔ **Come closer . . . closer:** Often, the most interesting shot is the one that reveals the small details.

Figure 5-2: One rule of composition is to divide the frame into thirds and position the main subject at one of the intersection points.

Figure 5-3: To add life to your images, frame the scene so that the eye is naturally drawn from one edge of the image to the other.

Posting viewer-friendly images

Large images, or several images on one page, can create a long download time, which is frustrating for the people trying to view your wares. Follow these ground rules for images that you post on the Web:

✔ Keep image size to a minimum — no more than 20K per picture and a total of 50K per page is optimal.

✔ Save your images in either the JPEG or GIF file format.

✔ Make sure that every image you add is *necessary* — don't junk up your page with lots of pretty pictures that do nothing to convey the message of your product.

✔ To accommodate the widest range of viewers, size your images with respect to a screen display of 640 x 480 pixels.

✔ Remember that anyone who visits your page can download, save, edit, print, and distribute your image. So if you want to control the use of your picture, don't post it on the Web.

Which came first, the digital camera or the scanner?

Which is better for capturing images — digital cameras or digital scanners? As with all gadgets, here's the classic answer: It depends.

You can't really beat a digital camera, but before you go snag one, decide what kind of investment (and how big) you plan to make in your online auctions. If you're already comfortable with 35mm camera equipment, don't scrap it — scan it!

Part III
The Part of Tens

The 5th Wave
By Rich Tennant

"It's amazing what a good search engine can locate. There's your car keys behind the sink and my ukulele in the basement."

In this part . . .

*L*ike going to the mall, the Internet can consume a great deal of time. And, also like the mall, the deals you find on the Internet can be expensive if you don't know where to shop. The chapters in this part will put you in that elite category of people who know how to find what they want quickly, and how to scan the Web for great deals. You'll find tips that will make you an expert shopper, and you won't have to troll for a parking space!

Chapter 6

Ten Search Engines for Online Research

*S*earch engines are programs that search large indexes of information gathered by robots sent out to *catalog* (sort and record) resources on the Internet. (*Robots* are programs that travel throughout the Internet and collect information on the various sites and resources that they run across.) You can access the information contained in search engines through an *interface* (a form or page online), usually through a form on a Web page. This chapter acquaints you with ten search engines to aid you in online living.

AltaVista

AltaVista (www.altavista.com) was the Web's first really deep search engine. Although it's no longer the only in-depth player out there, AltaVista is still a good starting point for a comprehensive search. AltaVista enables you to do the following:

✔ Search Usenet newsgroups as well as the Web

✔ Search in a couple of dozen languages other than English

✔ Look for people and businesses via the Switchboard directory service

✔ Browse by subject category, as well as run a regular keyword search

Ask Jeeves

Ask Jeeves (www.askjeeves.com) is a search engine with a twist. First, it attempts to find the answer to your plain-English question in its own vast collection of Internet resources. Figure 6-1 shows what happens when you ask Jeeves "Where can I find out about travel to New Zealand?" It displays a list of closely-matching questions that it understands. The first question happens to be an exact match, and when you click it, Jeeves takes you to a fine collection of New Zealand travel sites.

But, that's not all! Following the list of questions, Jeeves shows you a list of other search engines, that it's checked on its own — give that machine a bonus for initiative! — along with the number of hits for each one. You can browse all the hits by clicking the arrow to the right of each box, and go directly to the full results list at each site by clicking the search engine name.

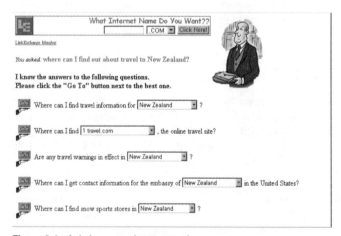

Figure 6-1: Ask Jeeves points you to the answers.

If you've seen one search engine, you've seem 'em all

Although each search engine has its own variations, all of them function similarly. All search engines have an interface with a form in which you enter keywords to search for in the search engine's index. Each search engine then runs a search of its index, returning its findings to you online with links directly to the pages where the search engine's robot identified the keywords.

Excite

Excite's (www.excite.com) main claim to fame is what it calls *concept searching.* Like other search engines, it looks for documents containing the search terms you supply. But it takes a giant step beyond that, linking your keywords to its own internal database of synonyms and related concepts, and then searching automatically for those terms and concepts as well. This extra step means that if you enter a keyword such as **teenager**, Excite looks for references to "adolescents," "youth," and "young people," as well. Amazing, isn't it?

After you run your search, Excite suggests additional words that you may want to include and lets you check any that you want to add. Excite also gives you a boost when you're having trouble narrowing down your search. If, while browsing your results, you find one or more items that are very close to what you're seeking, click the <u>More Like This</u> link. Excite uses the terms and concepts in that document as a model for your ideal answer, and refines your search accordingly.

HotBot

True to its slick, colorful graphics, HotBot (hotbot.lycos. com/) is a lean, mean, research machine. HotBot lets you

✔ Conduct several different kinds of specialized research right off the bat by restricting your search terms to certain Net resources, such as newsgroups and other discussion forums, current news sites, business and residential directories, e-mail listings (via a link to BigYellow), classified ads, stock quotes, and even Internet domain registrations.

✔ Use pull-down menus and check boxes to limit your search by date, geography, and media type (including images and multimedia).

✔ Restrict your search term to the title of a Web page.

✔ Tailor your search results by specifying how many items you want to browse at once, and whether you want to see full or brief descriptions.

Infoseek

Always a solid performer in the search engine sweeps, Infoseek (www.infoseek.com) is another good bet for a deep, fairly comprehensive search. Infoseek allows you to do the following:

✔ Search in French (*et voilà!*) as well as in English

✔ Search newsgroups as well as the Web

✔ Confine your search to wire services, industry journals, national newspapers, and other Web-based news sources — particularly helpful if you're looking for news stories or company descriptions

✔ Refine your search, after getting your first round of results, by clicking the **search only within these pages** button and entering some additional terms

Lineages Free Genealogy Queries

Lineages (www.lineages.com/queries/queries.asp) is a professional research service that offers free queries as part of its Web site. The surname queries are sorted by country or surname and Soundex. You enter queries by country — for example, if your ancestor lived in the United States, then you enter your query under the United States.

You're asked to provide your first name, last name, full address, phone number, fax number, e-mail address, and Lineages' account number (if you have one and know it). You can consult a section called "Write Successful Genealogy Queries" if you have any questions when posting your message. Your query should include the surname you're researching, additional surnames, message, locality, name, and e-mail address.

LookSmart Travel

At LookSmart (`www.looksmart.com`), you start with broad terms, such as travel and vacations, and drill down to specific terms, such as a specific destination. After you get to the country or city you're interested in, LookSmart presents you with a list of sites that relate to the topic.

Lycos World City Guide

Lycos World City Guide (`cityguide.lycos.com`) presents you with a clickable world map. Clicking the region you're interested in brings you to a more detailed map that eventually leads you to a city guide. This city guide contains a few paragraphs of descriptive text and a list of links broken down into categories. The links aren't necessarily exclusively for the city; they may pertain to the country as a whole.

Search.Com

Search.Com (`search.com/`) compiles research tools from hundreds of different sites Net-wide. You can search any of a handful of top search engines from Search.Com as well.

Check out the <u>A-Z List</u> of live links to get an idea of what's out there *beyond* the usual suspects: How about the <u>AmeriCom Long Distance Area Decoder</u>? <u>America's Job Bank</u>? <u>The Auto Trader Online Dealer Search</u>? And those are just a few of the **As**!

Yahoo! Travel

The Yahoo! travel section (travel.yahoo.com/) uses content from various well-known travel publications to give its travel section gusto. The destination info is the same that you find at the Lonely Planet Web site (www.lonelyplanet.com.au), but beyond that, Yahoo! provides current weather reports for most destinations, a frequently updated destination spotlight (by way of National Geographic Traveler), and pertinent articles courtesy of *Travel and Leisure* magazine.

Chapter 7

Ten Ways to Save Money on the Internet

*T*he Internet abounds with great deals, but — like great deals everywhere — you have to know how to find them. This chapter gives you over ten Web sites that offer money saving opportunities.

Flipping through Online Classified Ads

Online classified ads are a great means of tracking down individuals and organizations that have things to sell on the cheap. In fact, online classified ads are good places to look for all sorts of deals. You never know what you'll find:

✔ **Yahoo! Classifieds** (classifieds.yahoo.com)**:** From Yahoo!'s home page, click Classifieds near the top of the page. The listings generally contain a short description and the contact info for the supplier, including e-mail addresses.

Never give out your credit card number online until you know that a deal is legitimate.

  ✔ **Classifieds2000 (**www.classifieds2000.com**):**
    Classifieds2000 is an enormous database of classified
    ads for everything from real estate to pets. When you
    find what you're looking for, click the individual listings
    to access a description and seller info, as well as a form
    to contact the seller by e-mail.

Driving via Auctions

Ever wonder what the federal government does with all those
cars it takes from criminals? It sells them at federal car auctions. Go to eqmoney.com/cars.htm to find seized cars,
trucks, and boats that are available at incredible discounts.
You can't make a purchase online, but you can use this site to
get times and places where auctions will be held. What's
more, the "Guide to Federal Car Auctions" is free.

Lacing Up Your Traveling Shoes

Some of the best deals on the Web involve travel. If you'd
rather surf the waves in Honolulu than surf the Internet from
your living room, you'll find loads of good information on
travel bargains in this section.

E-mail newsletters

More and more travel sites are offering e-mail newsletters.
Although you definitely want to be careful about the number
of newsletter compilations you have flowing into your inbox
each day, you may find the following sites helpful in capturing
the elusive airfare discount:

  ✔ **Best Fares Magazine's Hot Deals by E-mail (**www.
    bestfares.com/e-deals/e-deal.htm**):** A must for any
    budget-conscious traveler. The leading budget travel
    magazine sends out this newsletter on a semi-regular,
    weekly basis. Hot Deals can be a terrific source of dis-
    count travel information.

- ✔ **The Air Travel Update:** This weekly newsletter compiles deals and bargains from all over the Internet. To subscribe, send an e-mail to `majordomo@listserv.prodigy.com` with the phrase **subscribe airtravel** in the body of the e-mail. (By the way, this newsletter comes highly recommended by John Levine, co-author of *The Internet For Dummies,* 7th Edition, published by IDG Books Worldwide, Inc., and an extremely knowledgeable online travel planner in his own right. Check out his Web site, *Airline Information on the Internet,* at `www.iecc.com/airline`.)

- ✔ **WebFlyer's Deal Watch** (`www.webflyer.com/@deal/@deal.htm`): Deal Watch isn't a newsletter, but rather a compilation of many airlines' weekly deals. Check in each week to search for domestic and international flights, hotel deals, and car rental promotions.

- ✔ **Smarter Living Travel Specials Newsletter** (`www.smarterliving.com/index.html`): *Smarter Living* apparently equates intelligence with bargain hunting skills — it sends out a weekly newsletter summarizing the airfare bargains for many airlines. Enter your e-mail address to subscribe to the newsletter.

- ✔ **Fare Wars Mailing List** (`www.travelersnet.com/farewars/index.htm`): Keep abreast of the latest airline fare skirmishes by subscribing to this mailing list. As soon as airlines lower their fares, you'll know about it.

- ✔ **The Cruise News Daily** (`www.reply.net/clients/cruise/cnd.html`): Published each day, this newsletter details the latest developments in the cruise industry, including new routes, new ships, and cruise promotions. To subscribe, follow the link on the main page entitled "E-mail Subscription to Cruise News Daily (free)" and then enter your e-mail address.

Hotel Reservations Network

Hotel Reservations Network (HRN) (`www.180096hotel.com`), Figure 7-1, has made a name for itself by doing one thing and doing it very, very well: providing rooms in great hotels in selected cities across the U.S. at low rates.

Figure 7-1: This site offers low rates at good hotels throughout the United States.

HRN's rates are amazingly low — sometimes up to 65 percent off the standard rate. They also can get rooms when a hotel tells you that it's sold out; HRN buys up blocks of hotels rooms at a wholesale price and then passes the savings on to you. It's awful nice of them. Just follow these steps to find out what HRN has to offer:

1. **Select the appropriate city from the list.**

2. **Enter the dates you want to stay.**

3. **Click Display Rates.**

   The search yields a list of hotels, with star ratings and nightly rates. You can get more info about a specific hotel and a map by clicking the corresponding buttons.

4. **Book the hotel online after you make a selection by inputting your personal and credit card information.**

   You can also call the toll-free number (it's part of the site's address) and speak to a representative seven days a week.

Not too difficult, huh? If you have any problem, the site posts its toll-free number all over the place, and you're encouraged to dial.

If you travel a great deal, sign up for the Hot Deals newsletter. Enter your e-mail address into the box on the home page, and you receive the newsletter of hotel deals the next time the site publishes it.

Click-It! Weekends

Waiting till the last minute to plan a trip has definite advantages in terms of its effect on your wallet. *Click-It! Weekends* (www.travelweb.com/TravelWeb/clickit.html), Figure 7-2, is a last-minute hotel room clearance service of TravelWeb, one of the premiere online hotel reservation systems.

Figure 7-2: The Click-It! Weekends site proves that procrastination can pay.

Click-It! Weekends provides a reliable way to get cheap hotel rooms in top-notch properties (mostly the big, global hotel chains — Hilton, Sheraton, and so on) around the world. Combine it with a last minute, discount flight and you've got yourself a cheap weekend getaway. Here's how the site works:

1. **A thrifty traveler, such as yourself, needs a place to stay for the coming weekend (Friday to Sunday).**

2. **On Monday you point your browser to** www.travel web.com/TravelWeb/clickit.html.

You can look at the site on any day, but the deals get scooped up quickly, so we recommend looking every Monday, which is when the site is updated.

3. **Click Locations (listings for hotels around the world) or Hotels and search the database to find discounted rates at a variety of major hotel chains.**

4. **Check availability by clicking the hotel link, selecting the arrival date and preferred bed size, and clicking Check Availability!**

   The site presents you with the available rates.

5. **Select the rate that best suits you and book the room online with a credit card.**

Arthur Frommer's BudgetTravel Online

Budget travelers should frequently check *Arthur Frommer's BudgetTravel Online* (www.frommers.com). Whether you're looking for inexpensive vacation packages, cruises, or discount tour operators, *Frommer's* can usually lend a hand. Go ahead and try the site's search function to search for keywords that apply to the trip you're planning.

Also of great value is Arthur's soapbox (http://www.frommers.com/soap_box/), where Frommer's lays his hard-won budget travel advice on you.

Frommer's has the market cornered on discount travel information and these days, that includes consolidators. *Consolidators* sell at deep discounts, which means deep savings for you. Go to (www.frommers.com/deals/hot_tickets/) to find out more.

Concierge.com

Each week, *Concierge.com* (www.concierge.com/travel/c_planning/04_deal/archive/intro.html) highlights a vacation deal of the week that is almost guaranteed to make your mouth water and your feet itch (in a good way). If the current trip o' the week doesn't strike your fancy, no worries, because the site offers an archived listing of past deals that are still current and available.

Index

Get it Done With Dummies
Bestsellers on Every Topic!

 ## TECHNOLOGY TITLES

INTERNET/ONLINE

America Online® For Dummies®, 5th Edition	John Kaufeld	0-7645-0502-5	$19.99 US/$27.99 CAN
Banking Online Dummies®	Paul Murphy	0-7645-0458-4	$24.99 US/$34.99 CAN
eBay™ For Dummies®	Roland Warner	0-7645-0582-3	$19.99 US/$27.99 CAN
E-Mail For Dummies®, 2nd Edition	John R. Levine, Carol Baroudi, & Arnold Reinhold	0-7645-0131-3	$24.99 US/$34.99 CAN
Genealogy Online For Dummies®	Matthew L. Helm & April Leah Helm	0-7645-0377-4	$24.99 US/$34.99 CAN
Internet Auctions For Dummies®	Greg Holden	0-7645-0578-9	$24.99 US/$34.99 CAN
Internet Directory For Dummies®, 3RD Edition	Brad Hill	0-7645-0558-2	$24.99 US/$34.99 CAN
Internet Explorer 5 for Windows® For Dummies®	Doug Lowe	0-7645-0455-X	$19.99 US/$28.99 CAN
Investing Online For Dummies®, 2nd Edition	Kathleen Sindell, Ph.D.	0-7645-0509-2	$24.99 US/$34.99 CAN
Job Searching Online For Dummies®, 2nd Edition	Pam Dixon	0-7645-0673-0	$24.99 US/$34.99 CAN
Travel Planning Online For Dummies® 2nd Edition	Noah Vadnai	0-7645-0438-X	$24.99 US/$34.99 CAN
World Wide Web Searching For Dummies®, 2nd Ed.	Brad Hill	0-7645-0264-6	$24.99 US/$34.99 CAN
Yahoo!® For Dummies®	Brad Hill	0-7645-0582-3	$19.99 US/$27.99 CAN

OPERATING SYSTEMS

DOS For Dummies®, 3rd Edition	Dan Gookin	0-7645-0361-8	$19.99 US/$27.99 CAN
GNOME For Linux® For Dummies®	David D. Busch	0-7645-0650-1	$24.99 US/$37.99 CAN
LINUX® For Dummies®, 2nd Edition	John Hall, Craig Witherspoon, & Coletta Witherspoon	0-7645-0421-5	$24.99 US/$34.99 CAN
Mac® OS 8.5 For Dummies®	Bob LeVitus	0-7645-0397-9	$19.99 US/$28.99 CAN
Red Hat® Linux® For Dummies®	Jon "maddog" Hall	0-7645-0663-3	$24.99 US/$34.99 CAN
Small Business Windows® 98 For Dummies®	Stephen Nelson	0-7645-0425-8	$24.99 US/$34.99 CAN
UNIX® For Dummies®, 4th Edition	John R. Levine & Margaret Levine Young	0-7645-0419-3	$19.99 US/$27.99 CAN
Windows® 95 For Dummies®, 2nd Edition	Andy Rathbone	0-7645-0180-1	$19.99 US/$27.99 CAN
Windows® 98 For Dummies®	Andy Rathbone	0-7645-0261-1	$19.99 US/$27.99 CAN
Windows® 2000 Professional For Dummies®	Andy Rathbone	0-7645-0641-2	$19.99 US/$29.99 CAN
Windows® 2000 Server For Dummies®	Ed Tittel	0-7645-0341-3	$24.99 US/$37.99 CAN

WEB DESIGN & PUBLISHING

Active Server™ Pages For Dummies®, 2nd Edition	Bill Hatfield	0-7645-0603-X	$24.99 US/$37.99 CAN
Cold Fusion 4 For Dummies®	Alexis Gutzman	0-7645-0604-8	$24.99 US/$37.99 CAN
Creating Web Pages For Dummies®, 4th Edition	Bud Smith & Arthur Bebak	0-7645-0504-1	$24.99 US/$34.99 CAN
Dreamweaver™ For Dummies®	Janine Warner	0-7645-0407-X	$24.99 US/$35.99 CAN
FrontPage® 2000 For Dummies®	Asha Dornfest	0-7645-0423-1	$24.99 US/$34.99 CAN
HTML 4 For Dummies®,2nd Edition	Ed Tittel & Stephen Nelson James	0-7645-0572-6	$24.99 US/$34.99 CAN
Java™ For Dummies®, 2nd Edition	Aaron E. Walsh	0-7645-0140-2	$24.99 US/$34.99 CAN
PageMill™ 2 For Dummies®	Deke McClelland & John San Filippo	0-7645-0028-7	$24.99 US/$34.99 CAN
XML™ For Dummies®, 2nd Edition	Ed Tittel	0-7645-0692-7	$24.99 US/$37.99 CAN

DESKTOP PUBLISHING GRAPHICS/MULTIMEDIA

Adobe® InDesign™ For Dummies®	Deke McClelland	0-7645-0599-8	$19.99 US/$27.99 CAN
CorelDRAW™ 9 For Dummies®	Deke McClelland	0-7645-0523-8	$19.99 US/$27.99 CAN
Desktop Publishing and Design For Dummies®	Roger C. Parker	1-56884-234-1	$19.99 US/$27.99 CAN
Digital Photography For Dummies®, 3rd Edition	Julie Adair King	0-7645-0646-3	$24.99 US/$37.99 CAN
Microsoft® Publisher 98 For Dummies®	Jim McCarter	0-7645-0395-2	$19.99 US/$27.99 CAN
Visio 2000 For Dummies®	Debbie Walkowski	0-7645-0635-8	$19.99 US/$29.99 CAN

MACINTOSH

Macs® For Dummies®, 6th Edition	David Pogue	0-7645-0398-7	$19.99 US/$27.99 CAN
Macs® For Teachers™, 3rd Edition	Michelle Robinette	0-7645-0226-3	$24.99 US/$34.99 CAN
The iBook™ For Dummies®	David Pogue	0-7645-0647-1	$19.99 US/$29.99 CAN
The iMac For Dummies®, 2nd Edition	David Pogue	0-7645-0648-X	$19.99 US/$29.99 CAN

PC/GENERAL COMPUTING

Building A PC For Dummies®, 2nd Edition	Mark Chambers	0-7645-0571-8	$24.99 US/$34.99 CAN
Buying a Computer For Dummies®	Dan Gookin	0-7645-0313-8	$19.99 US/$27.99 CAN
Family Tree Maker For Dummies®	Matthew & April Helm	0-7645-0661-7	$19.99 US/$27.99 CAN
Illustrated Computer Dictionary For Dummies®, 3rd Edition	Dan Gookin & Sandra Hardin Gookin	0-7645-0143-7	$19.99 US/$27.99 CAN
Palm Computing® For Dummies®	Bill Dyszel	0-7645-0581-5	$24.99 US/$34.99 CAN
PCs For Dummies®, 7th Edition	Dan Gookin	0-7645-0594-7	$19.99 US/$27.99 CAN
QuickBooks 2000 For Dummies®	Stephen Nelson	0-7645-0665-X	$19.99 US/$29.99 CAN
Small Business Computing For Dummies®	Brian Underdahl	0-7645-0287-5	$24.99 US/$34.99 CAN
Smart Homes For Dummies®	Danny Briere	0-7645-0527-0	$19.99 US/$27.99 CAN
Upgrading & Fixing PCs For Dummies®, 4th Edition	Andy Rathbone	0-7645-0418-5	$19.99 US/$27.99 CAN

Get it Done With Dummies
Bestsellers on Every Topic!

 ## TECHNOLOGY TITLES

SUITES

Microsoft® Office 2000 For Windows® For Dummies®	Wallace Wang & Roger C. Parker	0-7645-0452-5	$19.99 US/$27.99 CAN
Microsoft® Office 2000 For Windows®, For Dummies® Quick Reference	Doug Lowe & Bjoern Hartsfvang	0-7645-0453-3	$12.99 US/$17.99 CAN
Microsoft® Office 4 For Windows® For Dummies®	Roger C. Parker	1-56884-183-3	$19.95 US/$27.99 CAN
Microsoft® Office 97 For Windows® For Dummies®	Wallace Wang & Roger C. Parker	0-7645-0050-3	$19.99 US/$27.99 CAN
Microsoft® Office 97 For Windows® For Dummies®, Quick Reference	Doug Lowe	0-7645-0062-7	$12.99 US/$17.99 CAN
Microsoft® Office 98 For Macs® For Dummies®	Tom Negrino	0-7645-0229-8	$19.99 US/$27.99 CAN

WORD PROCESSING

Word 2000 For Windows® For Dummies®, Quick Reference	Peter Weverka	0-7645-0449-5	$12.99 US/$19.99 CAN
Corel® WordPerfect® 8 For Windows® For Dummies®	Margaret Levine Young, David Kay, & Jordan Young	0-7645-0186-0	$19.99 US/$27.99 CAN
Word 2000 For Windows® For Dummies®	Dan Gookin	0-7645-0448-7	$19.99 US/$27.99 CAN
Word For Windows® 95 For Dummies®	Dan Gookin	1-56884-932-X	$19.99 US/$27.99 CAN
Word 97 For Windows® For Dummies®	Dan Gookin	0-7645-0052-X	$19.99 US/$27.99 CAN
WordPerfect® 9 For Windows® For Dummies®,	Margaret Levine Young	0-7645-0427-4	$19.99 US/$27.99 CAN
WordPerfect® 7 For Windows® 95 For Dummies®	Margaret Levine Young & David Kay	1-56884-949-4	$19.99 US/$27.99 CAN
Word Pro® for Windows® 95 For Dummies®	Jim Meade	1-56884-232-5	$19.99 US/$27.99 CAN

SPREADSHEET/FINANCE/PROJECT MANAGEMENT

Excel For Windows® 95 For Dummies®	Greg Harvey	1-56884-930-3	$19.99 US/$27.99 CAN
Excel 2000 For Windows® For Dummies®	Greg Harvey	0-7645-0446-0	$19.99 US/$27.99 CAN
Excel 2000 For Windows® For Dummies®, Quick Reference	John Walkenbach	0-7645-0447-9	$12.99 US/$17.99 CAN
Microsoft® Money 98 For Dummies®	Peter Weverka	0-7645-0295-6	$24.99 US/$34.99 CAN
Microsoft® Money 99 For Dummies®	Peter Weverka	0-7645-0433-9	$19.99 US/$27.99 CAN
Microsoft® Project 98 For Dummies®	Martin Doucette	0-7645-0321-9	$24.99 US/$34.99 CAN
MORE Excel 97 For Windows® For Dummies®	Greg Harvey	0-7645-0138-0	$22.99 US/$32.99 CAN
Quicken® 98 For Windows® For Dummies®	Stephen L. Nelson	0-7645-0243-3	$19.99 US/$27.99 CAN

DATABASE

Access 2000 For Windows® For Dummies®	John Kaufeld	0-7645-0444-4	$19.99 US/$27.99 CAN
Access 97 For Windows® For Dummies®	John Kaufeld	0-7645-0048-1	$19.99 US/$27.99 CAN
Approach® 97 For Windows® For Dummies®	Deborah S. Ray & Eric J. Ray	0-7645-0001-5	$19.99 US/$27.99 CAN
Crystal Reports 7 For Dummies®	Douglas J. Wolf	0-7645-0548-3	$24.99 US/$34.99 CAN
Data Warehousing For Dummies®	Alan R. Simon	0-7645-0170-4	$24.99 US/$34.99 CAN
FileMaker® Pro 4 For Dummies®	Tom Maremaa	0-7645-0210-7	$19.99 US/$27.99 CAN
Intranet & Web Databases For Dummies®	Paul Litwin	0-7645-0221-2	$29.99 US/$34.99 CAN

NETWORKING/GROUPWARE

ATM For Dummies®	Cathy Gadecki & Christine Heckart	0-7645-0065-1	$24.99 US/$34.99 CAN
Building An Intranet For Dummies®	John Fronckowiak	0-7645-0276-X	$29.99 US/$42.99 CAN
cc: Mail™ For Dummies®	Victor R. Garza	0-7645-0055-4	$19.99 US/$27.99 CAN
Client/Server Computing For Dummies®, 2nd Edition	Doug Lowe	0-7645-0066-X	$24.99 US/$34.99 CAN
DSL For Dummies®	David Angell	0-7645-0475-4	$24.99 US/$35.99 CAN
Lotus Notes® Release 4 For Dummies®	Stephen Londergan & Pat Freeland	1-56884-934-6	$19.99 US/$27.99 CAN
Microsoft® Outlook® 98 For Windows® For Dummies®	Bill Dyszel	0-7645-0393-6	$19.99 US/$28.99 CAN
Migrating to Windows® 2000 For Dummies®	Leonard Stearns	0-7645-0459-2	$24.99 US/$37.99 CAN
Networking For Dummies®, 4th Edition	Doug Lowe	0-7645-0498-3	$19.99 US/$27.99 CAN
Networking Home PCs For Dummies®	Kathy Ivens	0-7645-0491-6	$24.99 US/$35.99 CAN
Upgrading & Fixing Networks For Dummies®	Bill Camarda	0-7645-0347-2	$29.99 US/$42.99 CAN
TCP/IP For Dummies®	Candace Leiden & Marshall Wilensky	0-7645-0473-8	$24.99 US/$35.99 CAN
Windows NT® Networking For Dummies®	Ed Tittel, Mary Madden, & Earl Follis	0-7645-0015-5	$24.99 US/$34.99 CAN

PROGRAMMING

Active Server Pages For Dummies®, 2nd Edition	Bill Hatfield	0-7645-0065-1	$24.99 US/$34.99 CAN
Beginning Programming For Dummies®	Wally Wang	0-7645-0596-0	$19.99 US/$29.99 CAN
C++ For Dummies® Quick Reference, 2nd Edition	Namir Shammas	0-7645-0390-1	$14.99 US/$21.99 CAN
GUI Design For Dummies®	Laura Arlov	0-7645-0213-0	$29.99 US/$42.99 CAN
Java™ Programming For Dummies®, 3rd Edition	David & Donald Koosis	0-7645-0388-X	$29.99 US/$42.99 CAN
JBuilder™ For Dummies®	Barry A. Burd	0-7645-0567-X	$24.99 US/$34.99 CAN
VBA For Dummies®	Steve Cummings	0-7645-0567-X	$24.99 US/$37.99 CAN
Windows® 2000 Programming For Dummies®	Richard Simon	0-7645-0469-X	$24.99 US/$37.99 CAN
XML For Dummies®, 2nd Edition	Ed Tittel	0-7645-0692-7	$24.99 US/$37.99 CAN